praise for

When we don't take the time to grieve in a healthy manner, it most assuredly will come out at a later, less opportune time, and in a more complicated fashion. No parent is prepared to grieve the loss of a child – it's not how it's supposed to be. The best person to speak into that wound is another who has similarly been wounded and has healed enough to have a sacred scar to show for it. Alycia Morales is that person – she loves hard, she grieves hard, and she offers hard-fought lessons from her sacred scars for *Surviving the Year of Firsts*. She understands because she's been there, and she offers every grieving mother a hand to hold.

Dr. Michelle Bengtson
Board Certified Clinical Neuropsychologist,
author of several award-winning books including *Sacred Scars: Resting in God's Promise That Your Past Is Not Wasted*, and host of the award-winning podcast, *Your Hope Filled Perspective*.

After losing a son three years ago, *Surviving the Year of Firsts*, showed me how I could continue in the grieving and healing process. The insights, wisdom, Scripture, and Spirit-filled content is a beautiful map to journey grief in our own way and understand God's love walks with us.

DiAnn Mills
author of *Lethal Standoff* - Tyndale
September 2024

Alycia Morales trusted in God as He walked with her through their first Christmas without Caleb. Through his first birthday in heaven. And through so many other "firsts" that break your heart all over again. Now she has taken what God taught her through those difficult times and put that in a book to help others through those moments of overwhelming grief. If you or someone you know is wading through grief, this book is a must.

Michelle Cox
bestselling author of *Our Daily Biscuit: Devotions with a Drawl and Hope That Endures*

Surviving the Year of Firsts resonated with me profoundly as someone who lost a child. I wish I had this book when I lost my son, Bryant, 20 years ago; the support and understanding Alycia offers in navigating a year of firsts would have been a precious gift. Her heartfelt reflections and the way she shares God's grace and strength provide such comfort and hope, reminding us that, with God, we can find strength and even joy again amidst our grief.

Jenae Alexander
Angel Mom, Author, Speaker, Nurse

As a mother who suffered the loss of my child, I took solace in the words of Alycia Morales in her book, *Surviving the Year of Firsts: A Mom's Guide to Grieving Child Loss.* She shares practical advice learned firsthand in the trenches of grief. This book will be a good companion to journey with you when surviving is often the only thing possible—and at times feels barely possible. Be encouraged that you will survive, and God will meet you along the path to provide comfort when you need it most.

Laura Hodges Poole
author of the upcoming *Waiting for Christmas,* an Advent devotional and follow-up to *While I'm Waiting* devotional

SURVIVING THE YEAR OF FIRSTS

A Mom's Guide to Grieving Child Loss

Alycia W. Morales

A Word In Season Publishing Company

Published by A Word In Season Publishing Company

Printed in the United States of America

Library of Congress cataloging-in-publication data is available upon request.

ISBN 979-8-9910005-0-5

eBook ISBN 979-8-9910005-1-2

Interior Design by Alycia W. Morales

Cover Illustration by Courtney Hopkins

Cover Design by Hannah Linder Designs

Photography by Alycia W. Morales

First Edition

dedication

to you, mama with the broken heart

I have stood where you stand. I pray you find hope and the ability to take one step forward every day until you find a smile comes with your tears and joy supersedes your grief.

contents

how to use this book

As I prepared for motherhood, I read all sorts of books on parenting. I learned about pregnancy and what to expect from week to week as my baby grew inside of me. I read about the differences I should anticipate when raising boys versus girls. Discipline tactics. Learning types. All sorts of things a mama needs to know when raising her first child.

I also heard that the pain childbirth brings with it is quickly replaced by the joy of holding your newborn close, smelling his or her sweet scent, and looking into the eyes of this masterpiece God has blessed you with.

What *no one* mentions in all that advice is that your child might die before you.

There aren't parenting books that say to be prepared to break wide open if your child beats you to heaven. They don't warn you that you're about to be forced to ride a roller coaster that plunges you into darkness and blinds you to what's coming around the next bend. That the highs and lows have a mind of their own, and you're just along for the ride.

Without Jesus, I don't know if I'd survive it. Even with Jesus, some days this ride is too much for me to bear, and I just want to curl up into a ball and hide from the world that keeps turning while my life has come to a sudden, jolting stop.

Mama, if you've lost a child, I want you to know you're not alone. I'm so sorry you have to walk this path in life. That you're on this journey that feels like it will never end. That you feel like you're on a terrible ride you can't get off.

As hard as it is to understand, and as much as you doubt it in this moment, I want you to know you *can* and you *will* survive the ride. You may never feel normal again; rather, you'll adjust to this new normal. But you will survive.

A few things to note:

My experience is viewed through my Christian faith in God the Father, Jesus Christ His Son, and the Holy Spirit. It is in my faith that I find hope and the strength to walk out this journey. It's from this viewpoint that I've written this book.

My husband Victor and I have been married for over twenty-five years. We have six beautiful children, five of whom survived the loss of their brother.

Vic and I now have three kids in heaven. Our 19-year-old son, Caleb, died in a single-car accident. We miscarried twice. And I have one (which makes four in heaven for me) that brought me into my relationship with Jesus. I will share that testimony in the pages to come, but please note this book focuses mainly on the loss of an older child. Although many of the topics covered could apply toward infant loss, the experiences I share throughout most of the book do not.

When we're grieving, we don't have a lot of time for anything more than surviving. Because of this, I kept the "chapters" short so you can read a little at a time and not feel overwhelmed. Each includes a survival tip (coping mechanism), a scripture verse, and a reflection question for you to answer. Whether or not you love to journal, sometimes it's therapeutic to just get your thoughts out on paper—to dump them, if you will. You may use your own journal or notebook to collect your thoughts, or you can use this free downloadable, printable journal I created just for you. You can find it at https://www.alyciawmorales.com/get-my-journal. It even comes with four covers to choose from!

hello grief

christmas 2020

2020 was a crazy year. Between Covid, social deprivation, and the American presidential election, it's a wonder any of us survived.

As the holiday season rolled around, our family looked forward to the year's end and a time of celebrating life together. Christmas of 2020 turned out to be the best Christmas any of us had ever experienced. Three years later, we still talk about the peace over that day.

What made it so different from Christmases before? If 2020 taught us anything, it's that we need to slow down more often, focus on family and friends, and live in the moment. Too often, we get busy with our careers and to-do lists and the kids' extracurricular activities, and we lose sight of what matters most: relationship.

We took the time that Christmas to stop worrying about buying all the gifts for all the people and only spent what we could afford. We focused on giving more than getting. We didn't worry about producing a huge meal and went with simple snack foods instead. Our feast became the laughter in our living room as we held our first White Elephant gift exchange. And we ended our day—and our year—rested.

As we approached January 1, 2021, like many others, we were hopeful that the new year would bring a respite from the crazy that 2020 was. Christmas Day seemed to prophetically establish that for our family, breathing a gentle sigh at the end of a long year. Little did we know what awaited ...

the phone call no mama wants to receive

The night of January 2, 2021, Victor and I were lounging on the couch like any other night of the year. We watched a movie while Vic laid in my lap scrolling social media, and I scratched his head with one hand and played a game on my phone with the other.

At 11:30PM, my phone rang. A local number appeared on my screen, and as I usually do, I ignored the call, suspecting spam. A moment later, I wondered who would spam call me that late at night. Immediately, the same number called again. This time, I answered.

"Is this the mother of Caleb Morales?"

My heart dropped. There are only two reasons an adult male would call and ask that question that late at night, and I knew my son wouldn't be in jail. "Yes."

"Ma'am, this is Officer ... accident ... Regional Hospital ... come to the ER entrance ... hurry."

My heart dropped another level. "Can you tell me his condition?"

"It's critical, ma'am. Do you know how to get here?"

"No." My mind wasn't processing anything more. My heart was now racing, and my eyes were watering.

The officer gave me directions. About three sentences in, I interrupted him. "Can you please tell my husband? He's driving." My focus shifted to getting out the door.

I phoned Mom. "Can you come over and stay with the kids?" They were all young adults and could have been home without us, but I feared the worst and didn't want them alone if I had to call with that news. Plus, two of my children suffer from severe anxiety. Hannah, only thirteen months younger than Caleb, would not handle this well at all. There was no way I was leaving her without an adult to cling to.

"Yes. What's going on?"

"Caleb had an accident. He's in critical condition. We have to go. Now." I eyed Vic as I told Mom.

We were out the door not two minutes later.

As we left our driveway, Caleb's fiancé called. "Where's Caleb?"

I could not tell her. I didn't know the details yet.

"Where's my baby?"

"Honey, let me talk to your mom."

She handed the phone over to Shawnna.

"We're on our way to the hospital. He's been in an accident. They're telling me he's in surgery and in critical condition. That's all I know. I don't know if they'll let you in or not, but please come."

"We're on our way."

When we arrived at the hospital, we were taken to a small room off the emergency waiting area, where the police officer met with us. "It appears he was driving too fast for the curve on bald tires on a wet road."

That's all the information we were given before being escorted to the dimly lit waiting room outside of surgery, where we spent the next two hours. At first, all I could do was sit and process. Then, all I could do was pace and pray. I made a few calls to request others we know and love to pray with us. Engelhardts. Millers. Helmses.

After about an hour and a half, around 12:45AM, I knew. There was this one split-second moment when I felt it in my heart —when I knew my baby had left this planet for Home.

A few minutes later, I only had the energy to sink to the cool floor and lean my head on a waiting room chair. No one had come out to tell us anything. No progress report. No good news.

Shawnna had texted and let me know they'd arrived but were having difficulty finding our location. They'd tried the ER, were sent to the front of the hospital, returned to the ER, and were finally on their way up.

I joined Vic on the bench.

At 1:30AM, a female in surgical scrubs emerged from the surgery wing. The expression on her face and tears threatening to spill over her cheeks said all I needed to know as I clung to Vic's arm.

"I'm so sorry. He died at 1:00AM. We knew how young he was, and we did everything we could to try to save him. He had a lot of internal bleeding, and we couldn't get it to stop. I'm so sorry. The entire surgical team is so heartbroken for you."

That guttural cry rose from within my husband and me at the same time, and we embraced as we wailed.

The attending surgical physician left us to our pain a few minutes later, just before Caleb's fiancé and her parents arrived in the waiting room.

I never again want to hear the cries of a 19-year-old when learning her beloved has just died. My heart died a little more as she cried out for her *Baby* and shook her head adamantly yelling, "No! No!"

We spent the next thirty minutes trying to survive the news. When we were finally able to pull ourselves together, we hugged goodbye and made plans to see each other the next day.

Vic and I didn't even make it to our vehicle before another wave of grief grabbed our hearts. We paused in the middle of the ER parking lot, wrapped our arms around each other, and cried. The ride home held an empty silence.

We had all joined a club none of us ever wanted to be members of.

I didn't sleep that night. Vic kept coaxing me to try to get some rest. Instead, I laid in bed with my eyes wide open, tossing and turning, imagining all sorts of scenarios at the scene of the accident, and grappling with my new reality.

My son is gone.

Too soon.

He wasn't supposed to beat me Home.

Life is out of order.

God, this hurts!

CHAPTER 1

One breath at a time

As I sat at my dining room table the life-altering Sunday that my son died, I caught myself unintentionally holding my breath. Multiple times, I reminded myself to breathe. *Something that came so naturally every other day of my life is now a struggle.*

Mama, as you experience day one of your year of firsts, take it one breath at a time.

Don't worry about all the things today. All the things can wait at least twenty-four hours. Give yourself a moment to grieve uninterrupted.

And breathe.

Survival Tip:

Try box breathing at least three times a day as needed, which may be every day for the entire year of firsts and then some. This deep breathing exercise has several benefits, including helping you refocus and find your calm.

- **Step One: Breathe in four counts (inhale).**
- **Step Two: Hold the breath four counts (pause).**

- **Step Three: Slowly release the breath four counts (exhale).**
- **Step Four: Pause four counts before repeating.**

The technique is also known as "square breathing."

While inhaling, picture God breathing His breath of life into you. When exhaling, release all the stress, anger, frustration, grief, and death—the things that will wreak havoc on your body if you keep them bottled inside.

Breathe in life. Exhale death.

A Verse to Focus On:

And the LORD God formed man of the dust of the ground and breathed into his nostrils the breath of life; and man became a living being.
Genesis 2:7

Reflection:

What is one thing you wish you could tell your child in this moment?

my last moments with my son

On the day of his passing, Caleb stopped by the house.
He'd moved out less than three months prior, renting a room in a friend's house. He and his fiancé were making wedding plans, and he wanted to prove to himself that he was stable and responsible enough to provide for his wife-to-be. That morning, he'd had plans with Vic and had come to meet his dad at the house.

Only Vic had gone to the range with Ezra and my dad, and I was at the store with Mom when Caleb arrived. He called me, asking where we all were. I told him I'd be there in about an hour and a half, and I asked if he wanted anything from the store and Zaxby's.

He asked for a bag of oranges and his Zaxby's "usual"—a six-finger plate tossed in original sauce, all fries, and a sweet tea. (That text is still on my phone.)

About an hour later, Mom and I finished shopping, went to Zaxby's, and headed home. Everyone else had already returned.

Caleb sat in his favorite spot at the kitchen counter and ate his food while I put away groceries, and we chatted. He hung out for half an hour before leaving to head to his fiancé's to spend time with her on her birthday.

I will never forget the hug he gave me that early afternoon. It lingered. He held on a little tighter. Looking back, it's as if he knew. *God* knew, at least. He squeezed me and said, "I love you, Mama." I responded with, "I love you too bud. I'm so proud of you."

And that was the last time I would see or hold him until eternity.

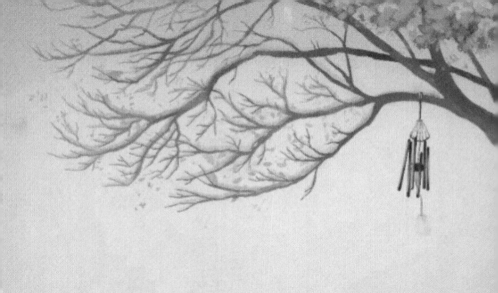

finding hope

CHAPTER 2

refreshing worship

I hadn't realized an entire week had blurred by since Caleb had passed until I prepared to attend church, where I fully expected to bawl my way through worship.

But God.

Instead of considering the loss of my son, I found myself focused on the fact that he was part of worship—experiencing worship—from one end of the earth to the other. That Caleb was participating with not only the heavenly hosts but us too. *Me too.* And that brought me incredible joy and a moment of sheer wonder.

We can only imagine ...

And he's living it.

Mama, it's so easy to focus on the end of your child's life. To let death catch your eye, your breath, and your heart. Don't allow those thoughts and emotions to swallow you up. This isn't the end for your child. It's the beginning. His or her birth into eternity.

CHAPTER 3

your purpose remains intact

M ore than once, I've questioned why God allowed me to
give birth to and raise Caleb just for him to make it
Home before me. What was the purpose in all of that? Because
sometimes it feels like there was no purpose to it all. He's just ...
gone.

*Does my purpose as his mother still exist without him? Do I still
have purpose? What happens if my other children die too? What
then, Lord?*

I have asked these questions and more since Caleb's passing.
I've sat in the moments of silent nothing wondering what to make
of all of this grief. Sometimes God has answered me. Sometimes
not.

One hard lesson I've learned over the years is that if I allow
motherhood to define me as a person, I will never be whole or
healed. I'll be missing out on far more than I could ask or think if
I limit myself to only being *Mom*. And when something happens,
like the death of a child, I'd likely be swallowed by grief because I
would have no other role to fulfill. No, motherhood is not *all* of
me. It's simply a large part of me and my life. But there's so much
more God has for me ... and you.

Mama, our main *purpose* in life is to bring God glory in all we say and do, representing Him as His ambassadors here on earth. Everything else we do is simply a *role*.

Most of these roles come and go with seasons in our lives. For example, our role as caregiver. This starts with our role as mother to our children then shifts to caring for our parents or spouse. One day, the role ends, but we remain in God's purpose.

Despite the loss of my son, my role as a mother remains. I will always be Caleb's Mama. He will always be a part of my life, and I have the hope of one day seeing him again. Until then, I will choose to walk in God's purpose.

Survival Tip:

Mama, consider all the facets that make up the gemstone of who you are. Start with the fact that you, like your child, were fearfully and wonderfully made in God's image and likeness (Psalm 139:13-14 and Genesis 1:26-27).

What other facets make up who you are? Are you a wife? Mama? Careerwoman? Homemaker? Daughter? Sister? Friend?

Who are you? What character traits did God pour into you? What's your personality like? What do you enjoy doing? What brings you joy? Sadness? What are you passionate about?

As you ponder these things, consider how they work toward fulfilling your purpose as a child of God. And how you're not limited to one role in life. Even when one is removed.

A Verse to Focus On:

*"I know that You can do everything,
And that no purpose of Yours can be withheld from You."*
Job 41:1

Reflection:

How can you use this grief journey to bring glory to God? How is it defining your purpose?

god is (still) good

Yes, Mama, the goodness of God is present in our lives, despite this struggle with grief. We must train ourselves to look for His blessings. Sometimes they're easy to spot. Other times, finding them depends on us focusing our vision and intentionally scoping them out when all we really want to do is curl up and avoid the day and all it holds.

Psalm 27:13 says, *"I would have lost heart, unless I had believed that I would see the goodness of the LORD in the land of the living."*

Without goodness, what do we have to live for? Did you know that the goodness of the Lord is attainable now? Today? In the land of the living? Even in the midst of death?

I have found it easy to allow my focus to dwell on the negatives of life: the loss of my son, marital struggles over the years, what I don't have that I feel I need, what isn't going right in my day. You get the gist.

Psalm 27:13 has seen me through many weeks. I have found the goodness of the Lord in the notes mailed by friends to encourage my faith, in the blessing of a check from my son's employer, in the DMV lady's whispered "You're doing great, Mama," as she snapped my daughter's photo, and in the moment when the Duncan PD Victim's Specialist took the time in the midst of his busy day to share his story of child loss with me.

In the face of death, especially that of a child, it's so easy to lose heart—to get lost in death. Seeking out the good in this life is a key to going forward on our journey toward surviving this trauma.

Survival Tip:

Tomorrow morning, make it a point to find the goodness throughout your day. Grab a journal, pull up a note on your phone, lay a piece of scrap paper on the kitchen counter. As you encounter the following, write it down.

- **Someone says or does something that blesses you.**
- **God's love for you is evident.**
- **You see something that touches your heart.** Like the sunrise or sunset, the joy in a child's eyes, or someone helping a stranger.
- **You hear a song on the radio or read a great line in a book.** And it ministers to you.
- **God illuminates a verse in His Word.** You know it's just for you in this moment.

At the end of the day, look back on your list and recognize the goodness you discovered in the land of the living. Choose to be thankful and recognize that despite the grief you suffer, there is still good in the world that makes life worth living every day.

A Verse to Focus On:

Surely goodness and mercy shall follow me
All the days of my life;
And I will dwell in the house of the LORD
Forever.
Psalm 23:6

Reflection:

What is one thing that truly touched your heart and brought you some much-needed healing today?

CHAPTER 5

eternal life

Some days grief feels like it's never going to go away. Like we'll be living under this weight of gloominess for the rest of our days. We end up questioning our faith as we wonder if hope will ever make an appearance. Will we ever see the light at the end of this never-ending tunnel?

As I spent time with the Lord one morning, my daily reading brought me to Psalm 23. This is the Psalm I memorized in Sunday school when I was eight. It's the Psalm I've read over and over and over again and am acquainted with. But I didn't know the depth of verse four until that particular morning.

> "Yea, though I walk through the valley of the
>   shadow of death,
> I will fear no evil;
> For You are with me;
> Your rod and Your staff, they comfort me."

Like God does, He brought this verse to life in my heart that day.

Grief can feel like you're walking through the valley of the shadow of death. Like grief's going to leap from the shadows and overwhelm you until you want to give in and give up. I know. I've felt that more than once in the past three years. But God opens His Word with a fresh revelation of His truth, and the shadow disappears.

A shadow is a dark area or shape produced by a body coming between rays of light and a surface. It's grief coming between the Light of the World and you. The good news is that a shadow is not a permanent darkness. As the light shifts, the body is no longer in the way and the shadow disappears.

This valley isn't permanent, because the shadow of death cannot sustain when we let the Light in. All we need to do is move position. We need to shift from sitting in our grief to standing in His presence.

Mama, death is not a permanent factor for the believer. It's not an end; it's a beginning. It's the entry into eternity with Christ if we have confessed our belief in Him as Lord and Savior and walked out our faith through the confession of our sins and repentance, living the rest of our days in obedience to Him.

Survival Tip:

To overcome the shadows, we have to shift our position, both internally and externally.

Internally, we need to adjust our perspective of this great loss we've suffered. If we don't, that shadow of death may supersede Jesus' light in us, tightening its grasp on our soul. A few ways to make that adjustment are:

- **Assess what you are choosing to believe.** Are you choosing to believe God took your child from you? Or are you choosing to believe death is a natural part of our lifecycle, and although it was untimely according to our world's standards, by God's grace your child went Home? Are you believing God is evil for allowing this tragedy in your life? Or are you believing that in His goodness, He will see you through it? If you need to, change your belief.

- **Admit the truth to yourself.** Mama, this one is not easy to do. You have to confront the lies the enemy would have you believe and expose them to the Light. God didn't kill or "take" your child. He is not to blame for your son's or daughter's death. Someone's sin, a disease or illness (physical or mental), or even an honest mistake is the reason for your child's passing. Truth hurts on the front end, but it frees us to be healed in every area of our lives if we will just confess it. It opens our hearts for God's forgiveness to take hold and work salvation miracles in us. If you need to, confess what truly took your child's life and ask God to forgive you for blaming Him.

Externally, we need to take our focus off ourselves and that shadow of death and allow light to shine through us. A few practical ways to do so are:

- **Return to the ancient paths.** What's a hymn or worship song from decades ago that has always ministered to your heart? Listen to it today, then share it on social media and let others know it's ministering healing to you. Maybe it'll touch someone else too.
- **Bring life to someone else.** Get out and do something worth doing. Volunteer at your favorite charity for a day. Visit a friend or family member who is shut in and take them a warm meal or a bouquet of fresh flowers.
- **Share the light.** Send another grieving mama a thinking-of-you card with an encouraging note. Let her know she's not walking this grief journey alone.

A Verse to Focus On:

Then Jesus spoke to them again, saying, "I am the light of the world. He who follows Me shall not walk in darkness but have the light of life."
John 8:12

Reflection:

What's one step you can take today to shift yourself out from under the shadow of death and step into God's glorious light?

CHAPTER 6

peace, be still

Caleb lived life to the fullest, fought to win, and strived for justice and fairness from the time he was old enough to talk. I don't think there was ever a time he wasn't standing up for something he felt was right or worth defending.

While I enjoyed watching him become strong in his physical strength and individuality, his personality flaws occasionally made him difficult to handle. As a toddler, he would attack his older brother. When I would encourage him to do what was right and leave his brother alone, Caleb would not relent. It usually took some type of physical force to pull him off of Ezra.

He wasn't good with change, either. As adults, we know how often we make plans only to have them cancelled because something else needs immediate attention. This type of change always sent Caleb into a tailspin.

While attempting to help my son better manage his emotions one day, that still-small voice of the Lord whispered, "Peace. Be Still." I always love when God intervenes with His wisdom. In that moment, I taught Caleb to still his inner turmoil with three simple words. *Peace. Be still.*

Sometimes we have to tell our flesh to settle down. When anxiety, fear, anger, frustration, or even grief rise up in us, raging like the storm the disciples found themselves fighting in Mark 4:35-41, we have to take charge and command peace. Tell the storm to be still. Make room for the great calm that follows.

Survival Tip:

Mama, when the storm of grief rises up in you, tell it to be still. When anger over your child's death threatens to overturn your faith and trust in the Lord, tell it to be still, in Jesus' name.

Just like forgiveness, sometimes it's difficult to feel the results of your decision to trust the Lord. Sometimes you need to speak out more than once or repeat it over and over in your heart until your flesh responds. That's okay. Just don't give up before the calm floods your spirit.

Here are a few ways I've found make it easier to lean into the peace that comes when we're still in the presence of the Lord:

- **Write in a journal.** Pouring my heart and thoughts out on paper always brings clarity and helps me push past those things that are weighing me down. Putting my emotions into words. Usually, I find my writing turns into prayer—a conversation with the Lord. And write down what He responds.
- **Put on worship music and simply listen or sing along.** Praise and gratitude turn doubt, depression, and difficulty into peace and joy if we allow it to. It helps to refocus our attention on the Lord of our life. Our Comforter.
- **Turn to the Word and find the truth.** When we're in emotional spirals, we tend to believe a lie, rather than seeking out the truth in the matter that set us off. I find the Psalms bring great comfort. The gospel of John, as well. There's no better way to calm a storm than to apply truth to the situation. And there's no greater source of truth than God's Word.

Survival Tip:

When death wants to seize your thoughts and squeeze your heart, say no.

- **Put on some worship music and sing through the tears.** Shift your focus back to the life your child is now living in eternity.
- **Focus on the firsts he or she is experiencing right now.** Rejoice as if you were watching her first band performance or ballet recital, his first soccer game or catching his first fish.
- **Keep singing through your tears until that smile sticks and your mindset shifts.**

A Verse to Focus On:

Let heaven and earth praise Him.
Psalm 69:34

Reflection:

What song brings you straight to the feet of Jesus?

A Verse to Focus On:

Be still, and know that I am God;
I will be exalted among the nations,
I will be exalted in the earth!
Psalm 46:10

Reflection:

What triggers the storm inside of you? Is it something someone says? The tone in which they say it? A song? Something you see? Knowing your response to these things is the first step toward calming the storm. Make a list of the things that trigger your grief and your responses to them.

he is my strength

Mama, every time I found out I was pregnant, I recognized that the child was God's first and that I was honored to be his or her mom. I also realized that He could take them Home at any moment, whether through their mistakes, the hands of another, or Father Himself (as in the case of Enoch). In those moments of meditating on the Word of the Lord and understanding His truths, I thought I'd be strong if that day came for one or multiple of my children. That I would stand strong in my faith in the God and that I would not turn to mush and fall apart.

The moment I learned that Caleb had gone Home to be with our Father, my strength evaporated. It melted away, leaving me barely able to sit upright, let alone stand or walk. Where I once felt like an oak tree, standing firm on solid ground, I felt like a puddle where every time someone stepped into my grief, more of me splashed out until I was drained of all I once was. In my own strength and will, I was weak. Have you felt this way?

Thankfully, God promises that when we are weak, He is strong (2 Corinthians 12:9-10). His Word tells us that He gives strength to His people (Psalm 29:11). That we can do all things through Christ who strengthens us (Philippians 4:13), including walk this grief journey with the One who is our very present help in time of trouble (Psalm 46:1).

I can see your eyes roll, Mama, when someone from the outside looks at you and what you're going through and tells you how incredibly strong you are. How amazed they are at how well you're handling this tragedy. Today I want to encourage you that in walking out your faith in God, putting your trust and hope in Him, leaning into Him for your strength, you *are* strong. Even in the midst of grief.

Survival Tip:

Mark 12:30 says, *"And you shall love the LORD your God with all your heart, with all your soul, with all your mind, and with all your strength.' This is the first commandment."* Just as we would go to the gym to do physical strength training, we can go to the Lord in our secret place to do spiritual, mental, and emotional strength training.

In an article for Psychology Today, Sarah Haufrect wrote, "To make a muscle stronger, it needs to become injured. It's only through the process of repairing damaged muscle fibers that growth takes place."[1] Mama, we're all suffering from broken hearts. Let's take a look at how we can work toward repairing our hearts in Christ and growing in our faith in this season with some spiritual strength training.

1. **Choose where you will work out**. Will you take a walk? Curl up in a favorite corner? Go to a local coffee shop or bookstore? Where is the best place for you to get undistracted time with the Lord?
2. **Choose your equipment**. What tools will you use to deep dive into your grief and God's Word? Which Bible do you prefer? Physical journal or electronic? Do you have a worship playlist or need to create one? Do you express yourself well with

some form of creative medium, such as paint or worship flags?

3. **Start light**. Increase slowly. Don't set yourself up for failure. Sometimes we tend to make big plans, and the first time we fail to follow through, we give up. Do you have five minutes in a day to spend in quiet time? That's fabulous! Start there! And increase slowly. Don't think that you'll jump from five minutes today to sixty minutes tomorrow. Slow and steady always wins the race.

4. **Pay attention to your pain**. Be aware of what you're feeling emotionally, mentally, physically, spiritually. Write it down. Work it out with the Lord. Don't ignore it, stuff it, or think that you're fine. It will only worsen with time if you don't address it today. Get help if you need it. Go for coffee with a mother or mentor. Call your spiritual advisor and schedule a time to meet. Get an appointment and talk with your therapist.

5. **Don't rush the process**. Have you ever turned up the heat on the oven to force something to bake faster? What happens? It burns. Or it comes out well-done on the outside and raw on the inside. Don't rush the process. Allow God and yourself the time to do a complete work within you. It will be worth the wait.

6. **Build in rest**. It's important to rest in the Lord. Martha kept going and going and going, while Mary sat at Jesus' feet. Jesus is our Sabbath rest. Make sure to take the time to enjoy resting in Him.

7. **Seek variety.** Doing the same thing over and over and over again day after day, month after month can get boring and tiring, which will only cause you to want to quit or will lead to actually quitting. Instead of focusing on one way of spending your quiet time, try mixing it up. Rearrange the order of your routine, try

a different time of day, use paper and pen instead of your phone, choose new songs to add to your playlist, go for a walk instead of staying inside. It doesn't have to be a major change, just something to encourage your spirit to awaken to what the Lord has in store for you.

8. **Focus.** Make it a point to focus on the Lord in this season. Grief, as you well know, can trigger all kinds of mayhem on our bodies, minds, and spirit. It can keep us from walking with the Lord as easily as it can drive us to Him. God can handle all your extra. Take it to Him. Don't hide from Him in your grief.

9. **Breathe.** As I said from day one, breathe in the life-giving breath of God. Breathe out the grief and death that would wreak havoc on your life if left unchecked. Let God fill you with His strength, so you can carry on in this abundant life.

A Verse to Focus On:

Whom have I in heaven but You?
And there is none upon earth that I desire besides You.
My flesh and my heart fail;
But God is the strength of my heart and my portion forever.
Psalm 73:25-26

Reflection:

What is one way you can draw nearer to God in this season of your grief journey?

CHAPTER 8

joy is okay

Throughout the first year after Caleb's death, I struggled to find joy in the midst of celebrations. Birthdays, graduations, weddings. As much as I tried to smile and enjoy these events, to be happy for the ones celebrating them, joy eluded me. Instead, I faced the grief of what could have been for Caleb and myself. I had the joy of watching him graduate from high school, but I wished he was there to celebrate Hannah's. I still have five kids, but I'll never get to be Grandma to those he may have had. You get the idea.

This isn't the only way grief tries to rob us of joy. One thing I discovered as I've scrolled social media groups for parents who've suffered child loss is that many mamas struggle with guilt over having happy moments in life, as if it dishonors their child.

Mama, you have a right to be happy in life. Not everything has to be overshadowed by your grief. Celebrating life is necessary if we are to continue in hope. I'm also certain your child would want you to be happy, just as they preferred you happy when they were still here.

Did you know there's a difference between happiness and joy? Happiness is an emotion based upon the current circumstances in our lives. When things go well, we are often happy. When they fall apart, happiness evades us as other emotions set in. Joy, on the other hand, is given by God and is based on our salvation, rather than our circumstances.

In Psalm 51:12, David proclaims, *"Restore to me the joy of Your salvation, and uphold me by Your generous Spirit."* Joy is something that nothing and no one can take from a believer, as we find in John 16:22. It's something God gives, a fruit of the Spirit. When we live in Him, we have continual access to joy.

So even when I have to remind myself what joy feels like, what joy sounds like, what joy looks like minute by minute throughout my battle with sorrow and grief, I know it is present within me. Because He is present with me. And despite my son's physical death, Caleb lives on in my heart as well.

Survival Tip:

Mama, one thing I've discovered in my faith walk is that when God has a destination for me, there will always be trials and tribulations along the way to getting there. Like the disciples in the boat, we have to battle the storms of life as we travel toward the place God has called us to.

Forgiveness, fighting the battles with our flesh, and healing take concentrated effort. So does unearthing that joy we're promised. These all require repetitive action. Practice. It only gets easier when we make a point of obtaining the prize or achieving the goal rather than allowing fear, anxiety, sorrow, grief, or any other thing to keep us in the storm.

One way to practice maintaining joy in your heart and reacquiring the ability to celebrate life is to leave Scripture around your home, putting it in places you frequent, such as the refrigerator, entryway, bathrooms, and bed. Below are a few you could write or print out:

Those who sow in tears
Shall reap in joy.
Psalm 126:5

Now may the God of hope fill you with all joy and peace in
believing, that you may abound in hope by the power of the Holy
Spirit.
Romans 15:13

You will show me the path of life;
In Your presence is fullness of joy;
At Your right hand are pleasures forevermore.
Psalm 16:11

On the natural side of life, we can practice joy by allowing ourselves to be present in the moment. Rather than living in the grief of the past and the what-should-have-been, choose to focus on the one you're celebrating—the birthday boy, the bride, the new parents. If your child's memory comes up, or grief tries to pull your focus away, choose to consider the joy your child would want you to experience in this moment, at this event. And allow yourself the grace to enjoy it.

A Verse to Focus On:

The Spirit of the LORD GOD is upon Me,
Because the LORD has anointed Me
To preach good tidings to the poor;
He has sent Me to heal the brokenhearted,
To proclaim liberty to the captives,
And the opening of the prison to those who are bound;
To proclaim the acceptable year of the LORD,
And the day of vengeance of our God;
To comfort all who mourn,
To console those who mourn in Zion,

To give them beauty for ashes,
The oil of joy for mourning,
The garment of praise for the spirit of heaviness;
That they may be called trees of righteousness,
The planting of the LORD, that He may be glorified.
Isaiah 61:1-3

Reflection:

What brings you great joy in this season, despite the sorrow?

caleb's gift

Caleb had recently—very recently—begun writing worship songs.

A couple of weeks before he moved out of our home, he'd popped into my room with his guitar in hand. "Mama, I'm writing a song. Check this out." He'd strummed the chorus. It was all he had at the time. In retrospect, I wish I had recorded him playing so we had the music. I'm not sure why I didn't. I usually record my kids every chance I get.

The week he died, we found out he'd written the entire song. Our youth pastors were in touch with a member of our church whom Caleb worked with at Roebuck Landscaping. Apparently, he'd finished the song on December 29th, less than a week before his death, and he'd shared the lyrics with his friend from work.

I am still so incredibly, deeply blessed by this. It was God's confirmation to my heart that our son had truly made Him his Lord and Savior and that he was Home. Our worship leaders at Hope Spartanburg put the lyrics to music and performed Caleb's song at his Celebration of Life.

Mama, I want to share his lyrics with you. God had recently done some amazing work in my son's heart. We have a video of the performance by our worship leader, and at one point you can hear

Caleb's oldest brother, Zachary, say, "Mission accomplished." Here's why:

Father I Come (to You)

Father I come to You broken and ashamed
Not the man I'm supposed to be and I wanna
* change my ways*
So Father I come to You with my broken promises
And the chains around my feet
It's time to let them go

Father I come to You with the songs of yesterday
But I'll leave them all behind
And I'll look toward Your face

Father I come to You
There's nothing I want more
I come to You

Father I come to You as a brand-new man
I lean into Your strength

©2020 Caleb Isaac Morales

survival self-care

CHAPTER 9

prioritize self-care

Self-care may sound selfish. It starts with the word self, doesn't it? Prioritizing your needs does not make you selfish unless you're solely focused on yourself. Let me present it this way: If you're on an airplane that's about to crash, is it selfish to put on your mask first so you can help others who need it? No. You aren't able to help others if you're worn-out tired, only seeing the negative in life, or ill. Taking care of yourself so you can care for others is imperative in this season.

Mama, you just went through one of the most traumatizing experiences a woman can go through. Your body is reacting in ways you never imagined. You can't remember what you had for breakfast, let alone what bills are due this week or who has what appointment coming up. Your emotions are all over the place, and you may even be questioning your faith.

One afternoon during the week of Caleb's Celebration of Life, I went out to my truck to retrieve something from the back seat. As I opened the door, the world started going black. Thankfully, I was able to shake my head and snap out of it before I passed out.

A few months later, I rose from the couch, where I'd been sitting all morning, and in the short walk between rooms, I felt like I couldn't breathe, my heart raced, and I once again thought I might pass out.

Emotionally, I was in an okay place those days. Spiritually, I remained strong in my faith in God and His plan in all of this. But my body knew the stress I was under and had its own ideas of how to make me aware of it.

That afternoon, I went to the emergency room. Grief can present physically with symptoms of a heart attack. Thankfully, my EKG came back normal. But my blood pressure was high, and the doctor ordered a stress test to be sure I was okay. The stress test came back normal as well. Final diagnosis? Hypertension.

And God has revealed why. Too much comfort food. Fried chicken. French fries. Sweet tea. Donuts. Daily trips through the drive thru lane and a lack of daily physical activity. James 4:17 says, *"Therefore, to him who knows to do good and does not do it, to him it is sin."* If I know I'm supposed to eat according to God's plan, and I eat according to my own plan, it's sin. Running to food for comfort instead of running to God is the sin of idolatry. I've placed food above Him in my heart. I've had to repent daily. It's been the biggest struggle between my flesh and spirit these past few years.

Self-care is of the utmost importance while we're walking out our grief journeys. Our families need us. God still had plans for our lives. And we need to be healthy in order to accomplish His will.

Survival Tip:

Take the time to do what you need spiritually, physically, mentally, and emotionally.

- **Use the bereavement days your employer allows you to take**. All of them.
- **Choose at least one healthy food a day**. Even when you're ordering takeout. Most fast-food restaurants

have some type of salad. Pair it with your burger and fries so your body is getting some healthy fuel. Do your best to avoid sugar and too much salt.

- **Drink half your body weight in ounces of water each day.** This will help flush your system of inflammation and stored fat, along with keeping you hydrated.
- **Take a walk.** Find a friend to walk with you or use the time to be alone and reflect.
- **Get some sunshine.** Vitamin D is your friend. Stand in the sunlight for ten to fifteen minutes per day several times per week. Sunlight helps keep your circadian rhythm functioning properly, which helps you ...
- **Sleep.** Try to get six to eight hours each night. Take naps as needed. Have hubby get up with the kids Saturday morning and allow you to sleep until noon. Allow him the same courtesy the following weekend. You may need more sleep in the early months of this new season of life as your body recovers from the shock of your loss.

A Verse to Focus On:

Do you not know that you are the temple of God and that the Spirit of God dwells in you? If anyone defiles the temple of God, God will destroy him. For the temple of God is holy, which temple you are.
1 Corinthians 3:16-17

Reflection:

What's one thing from the list above that you will implement in order to take care of yourself today?

CHAPTER 10

focused faith

Mama, in this first-year season, your faith will be tested. There will be days you will question the Lord. You'll wonder what God's plan is in the midst of this great loss you're suffering. Maybe you've already thrown a fist in the air and blamed Him for taking your child from you.

The week of Caleb's funeral, his fiancé came to us with a request that required stepping out in our faith and trusting God's response, regardless of whether or not it lined up with our hearts' desires. She wanted us to pray for God to raise Caleb from the dead.

Vic and I believe in the Resurrection Power of Jesus Christ. If God could use a prophet to pray breath and life into dry bones in a valley, raise Lazarus from the dead, and so many more miracles, He could certainly raise our boy back to life at any point before the funeral ended and he was buried. And I looked at his coffin more than once during his Celebration of Life, watching ... expecting ... hoping ...

Faith is the substance of things hoped for and the evidence of things *not seen* (Hebrews 11:1). Faith looks with supernatural eyes. Faith sees things that aren't so in reality. Faith believes that God means every word He speaks and writes. And if we were meant to do more than Jesus did when He was here, we could pray and prophecy life for the dead as well.

Then it's up to God to make the miracle happen.

Regardless of His answer, Mama, we must choose to continue to walk in our faith and trust God's goodness. Our children may not be alive here on earth, but they are fully alive in eternity with the Lord. And in that, we can find peace.

Don't beat yourself up for questioning God or having a lapse in your faith or doubting Him. He is bigger than your questions, and He has given you a specific amount of faith that will help you move mountains of doubt. Ask Him your questions. Tell Him your concerns. Thankfully, we serve a God who is fully alive and responds to His children.

Survival Tip:

To this day, I must continually shift my focus from my desires on earth to God's heavenly and eternal perspective. I only know His plan in part, but you and I can find peace and hope in knowing that one day, we will know it in full (1 Corinthians 13:12).

I encourage you to shift your focus from the death of your child on this earth to his or her eternity in heaven and God's plan in all of it.

- **Pause your thoughts.** When you find yourself mired in thoughts about your child's passing, stop the emotional onslaught. Take a deep breath.
- **Refocus on Jesus.** He conquered sin, disease, and death itself. Focus on life. What part of God's plan for your child here on earth could God now be fulfilling in heaven?
- **Think of one thing you can do today to honor God and to honor the life your child lived.**

- **Convince your heart and mind *you* will live again.** Focus your thoughts on John 11:25-26. *Jesus said to her, "I am the resurrection and the life. He who believes in Me, though he may die, he shall live. And whoever lives and believes in Me shall never die. Do you believe this?"*

A Verse to Focus On:

Finally, brethren, whatever things are true, whatever things are noble, whatever things are just, whatever things are pure, whatever things are lovely, whatever things are of good report, if there is any virtue and if there is anything praiseworthy—meditate on these things.
Philippians 4:8

Reflection:

What's something you can think upon that shifts your focus from death to life?

CHAPTER 11

sabbath rest

Prior to Caleb's passing, I was able to clean my entire house in a weekend. Since then, it's been a miracle if I've made it through cleaning an entire room in the same amount of time. There are other things I struggle to do. Like climbing more than the average flight of stairs or hiking.

These days, those activities leave me huffing and puffing like a dragon with asthma. Retrieving words I've known since middle school from the reserves of my brain is like trying to solve a common core math problem three different ways. Even creativity is a challenge. I haven't picked up a paintbrush in over a year. It's not that I don't desire to do these things. It's that I can't find the energy to do them.

Mama, you aren't going to have the energy to do all the things you normally do. Just as it did for me, the day is going to come when you are going to realize just how tired you really are. You need to allow your body time to heal as much as you need to let your heart heal. You need rest.

Rest isn't just a good idea; rest is a commandment. In Exodus 20:8-11, the Lord reminds us how for six days He created the heavens and the earth and all within them. Then, He rested. He

SURVIVING THE YEAR OF FIRSTS

commands that on the Sabbath day, we do not work. It's a day to take a break. To stop and consider His goodness. To rest in Him. This rest comes with benefits, which include improved physical, mental, relational, and spiritual health.

Rest may look different for you than it does for me. I enjoy binge watching shows or movie series while I lounge around in my pajamas and sip on a beverage until my eyelids are droopy and sleep engulfs me. You may prefer to take a walk, read a book, create something, or go axe throwing. Whatever rest looks like to you, be sure to make the time and do it.

Note: The world will keep spinning while you take a day off. If you need to, ask for help with the kids or the housework so you can take a much-needed break. Delegate things you know others can do in your stead. And get some sleep. You know you need it.

Survival Tip:

There are many ways you can set yourself up for a successful Sabbath rest:

- **Plan for a family and friends dinner.** Prepare the day before. Set up your crockpot or prep your InstaPot and keep the insert full of ingredients in the refrigerator overnight. Turn it on first thing the morning you plan to rest. You won't have to cook that day, and gathering around the table is something rare in our busy, microwave world.
- **Prioritize what is important.** Family and friends—relationships—are what matter most to the Lord and should matter most to us. Make relationship building a priority on your Sabbath, whether it's your relationship with the Lord, your family, or your friends.
- **Limit activities.** This is not the day to catch up on work you missed, cleaning house, or sorting through

the closets. Today is the day to do something that brings you closer to the people you love. Have everyone write an activity they would like to do together on a slip of paper. Put all the slips into a jar, bowl, or hat and draw one to do that day. Each Sabbath, draw a new one until each family member or friend's activity has been chosen. This makes everyone feel important to one another and allows everyone the opportunity to do something they enjoy, rather than something only one of you may like doing.

- **Set aside electronics for the day.** Put your ringer on silent. Turn off social media. Don't check your email. Spend face time with one another. Teach your children the art of having a conversation and allowing others a turn to express themselves without interruptions. Make the only exception be the opportunity to watch a movie or show with one another. Then have a discussion about what you've observed.
- **Leave time for a nap.** Sabbath is the perfect day to catch up on some of the sleep you've likely missed throughout the week. Take thirty minutes to get some shuteye. Your brain will thank you, and you may find you're more productive and creative during the week after taking a Sabbath rest.

A Verse to Focus On:

And He said to them, "Come aside by yourselves to a deserted place and rest a while."
For there were many coming and going, and they did not even have time to eat.
Mark 6:31

Reflection:

What's one way you will implement rest this week? Once you've
practiced rest, come back and write about how you felt afterward.

golden gratitude

Mama, Caleb's sudden loss left me feeling out of control, because I had no control over any of it. I wasn't present. I wasn't given time or opportunity for closure. *I didn't get to say goodbye.*

Rather than focus on that, I forced myself to shift my thoughts to what I was grateful for. Grateful he wasn't left here, suffering. Grateful he wasn't paralyzed or otherwise physically or mentally handicapped as a result of his car accident. Grateful to God for taking Caleb Home. Grateful God has fully healed my son.

The struggle is real. The dichotomy of emotions is strange. The brokenness inside of you feels like it will never become whole again. All of these can make it difficult to be grateful.

The Japanese have an art form called Kintsugi. Instead of throwing away the pieces, they take broken pottery and repair it by mending the cracks with lacquer that's been dusted or mixed with powdered gold, platinum, or silver.[1]

Tiffany Ayuda, in an article about how Kintsugi can help us deal with stressful situations, wrote, "Sometimes in the process of repairing things that have broken, we actually create something more unique, beautiful and resilient."[2]

What if God is taking your broken heart and creating something more unique, beautiful, and resilient in you? Psalm 147:3 says, *"He heals the brokenhearted and binds up their wounds."* Can you picture God taking your broken heart and binding that wound with something precious, like gold?

Mama, if you can't find something within your child's death to be grateful for, you can at least be grateful that God doesn't leave us in our brokenness. He brings His healing balm and binds up the wounds, making us whole again.

Survival Tip:

Take the time today to create something from your brokenness, whether you feel you are creative or not. We all have the power within us to create something. What do you enjoy doing? What brings you peace? What refreshes and restores you?

Here are some ideas to get you thinking about what you can create today:

- **Take a walk.** Pick a bouquet of wildflowers or autumn leaves, collect rocks, or find something in the shape of a heart to remind you of God's love for you and your child.
- **Spend time in your kitchen.** Bake your favorite dessert or whip up a new recipe. Enjoy it alone or invite your family to partake of it with you.
- **Whisper a prayer of gratitude**. Don't be afraid to express your hurt even as you are thankful.
- **Create time for yourself.** Take a few moments to do something that quiets your soul. Put bubbles in the bathtub and soak or light some candles and curl up with a good book. Go for a run or grab the fishing gear and head for the river.

The point is to create something from your brokenness.

Allow the healing process to work through this moment of creativity. And find something to be grateful for in the midst of it.

A Verse to Focus On:

I will offer to You the sacrifice of thanksgiving,
And will call upon the name of the LORD.
Psalm 116:17

Reflection:

What is one thing you wish you had control over regarding your child's death?

CHAPTER 13

speak life

Mama, how many times have you said out loud to yourself, "I'm so tired."? I know I've said it at least once a day for the past three years. Because even on the good days, I feel tired. When Caleb died, I think I aged ten years overnight. Nothing in my body works like it used to.

I used to laugh and tell people that my kids took something from me when they were born. Hannah took my gall bladder. Gideon took two of my teeth. And every one of them took some of my brain cells, I swear.

I believe I could say that Caleb's death took far more out of me than any birth, or even the two miscarriages I had. My brain is frequently foggy. My eyesight has decreased. My heart still aches with sharp pains every now and then, especially when my thoughts turn to Caleb. My back is sore more than it isn't. And I just feel run down and tired all the time.

After telling myself and God how tired I was one afternoon, the Holy Spirit reminded me that my tongue holds the power of life and death, blessings and curses. That I could speak tiredness over myself, or I could change my words to something more positive. Scripture, perhaps. Instead of declaring how tired I am, I can declare how I can do anything through Christ who strengthens me (Philippians 4:13). That when I am weak, I am strong because of Him (2 Corinthians 12:7-10).

Survival Tip:

Mama, we must watch our words, just like we remind our kids to do. We must stop speaking negative things over ourselves and begin to proclaim God's truths instead.

- **Take every thought captive to Christ (read 2 Corinthians 10:4-5).** Rather than saying the negative words you're about to speak, pause. Consider the opposite of what you're thinking. What does God's word say about that topic? What is the truth? His truth, not your own. You've just taken that thought captive and not allowed the enemy power over your tongue. Now, speak His truth.
- **Change your attitude.** Surrender your Negative Nelly to an attitude of gratitude. Take your focus off your pain, grief, or lack of energy. Silence the grumbling inside of you. What do you have to be thankful for today? Even if it's as simple as a warm cup of coffee, the smile on a child's face, or the gentle spring rain watering the earth outside your window, find something to be thankful for. Then, verbally express your gratitude toward God. After all, He created those coffee beans, that child's smile, and the rain. I can always find something in creation to be thankful for. I bet you can too, Mama.

If you're really struggling to focus on the positive in your life, try the following:

- **Write personal reminders on sticky notes or**

index cards. Post them around your home, office, car, or wherever else you find yourself.

- **Record a message on your phone.** Play it back when you need to be encouraged to think positive thoughts.
- **Decorate your home with Scripture or nature artwork.** Reflect on God's glory when you consider them.

Stop telling yourself and the spiritual realm that you're done. God has much more abundant life in store for you to enjoy. And you will enjoy it sooner than you imagine.

A Verse to Focus On:

A man's stomach shall be satisfied from the fruit of his mouth;
From the produce of his lips he shall be filled.
Death and life are in the power of the tongue,
And those who love it will eat its fruit.
Proverbs 18:20-21

Reflection:

What's something negative you've been speaking over your life since your child passed? What is God's truth about that particular thing?

CHAPTER 14

say no

Our family traditionally gathers for major holidays. My sister hosts Christmas, and we host Easter and Thanksgiving. When Easter rolled around in 2022, I looked forward to having the family gather in our home and to spending the day cooking and fellowshipping. Making the meal went fairly well. It wasn't until we sat down to eat that I realized I may have bitten off more than I could chew. By then, I was drained and just wanted to cry, lay down, and take a nap.

Mama, you may want to do all the things you've been doing your entire adult life. You may want to host a family gathering, go on an annual vacation, spring clean your home, or attend that company event. Your girlfriends may ask you to get away with them, or you may be invited to speak in front of a large group of ladies. The question is, will you be up for it?

Being able to say "no, thank you" without feeling guilty is a skill you need to develop in this season of grief. There's no shame in admitting you just aren't up for things. Grief is not a gentle companion. Rather, it takes more out of us than we realize until we've said yes and are in the middle of cooking for eighteen people. It's better to say no and allow yourself to rest than to say yes and find the cost too expensive.

While we were enjoying our ham, mashed potatoes, and glazed carrots, I announced I wouldn't be hosting Thanksgiving dinner that year. Thankfully, I have a mom and sister who are deeply understanding and agreed that I didn't need to exert myself in that season.

I encourage you to recognize your limits, set healthy boundaries, and say "no" when you're asked to do something you know will suck from you the little bit of life you're struggling to hold onto.

Survival Tip:

Mama, in order to maintain what little sanity you may have this year, you need to be able to put your foot down when family and friends think you should be able to do more than you know you're capable of doing. Don't allow them to weary you into over-committing yourself. Do the following instead:

- **Make a list of your priorities.** What are the most important things to you right now, in this current season of your life? The death of a child tends to rearrange our priorities. We quickly discover what truly matters and what we've been doing that wastes our time and energy.
- **Practice saying "no."** If you're a people pleaser, this may be difficult for you to do. But if I've learned one thing from the death of my child, it's that normal changes quickly, and I'm not the person I was prior to his accident. I am acutely aware of my limits. It's become a lot easier for me to decline an invitation when I know that event will wear me thin.
- **Set boundaries.** Make a list of things you're willing to do and things you're not willing to do. When someone asks you, be prepared to let them know that you've chosen not to participate in those things for a

period of time due to your current grief process. For example, I took time off from serving on the nursery team at church. Then I took time off from serving our youth group. Our family needed my focus and became the priority. And I was too tired to do much else for a season.

- **Don't listen to those who try to persuade you to say "yes" because they feel you should be "over that" by now.** Grief is different for everyone. And if they haven't lost a child, they truly have no clue what you're going through or how long it takes to heal from that trauma in your life. Just smile and tell them you're grateful they thought of you, but that you'll need to decline this time. And maybe next time too.
- **Let others host the holidays, serve on the teams, and take the trips for now.** One day, you'll be ready to do those things again. Until then, there's no guilt or shame in needing to rest.

A Verse to Focus On:

But let your 'Yes' be 'Yes,' and your 'No,' 'No.'
Matthew 5:37

Reflection:

What's the one thing you need to say no to right now, for this season?

CHAPTER 15

relationships matter most

Once I had Caleb's few belongings back at the house, I
wanted to bless his friends and family with a small piece of
his estate, which consisted mostly of clothing, Legos, and guitars.
As I planned who would be gifted my son's belongings, I
pondered how many times I'd purchased toys we threw away,
donated, or sold years ago, rather than saving those funds for a
memorable vacation. Suddenly aware that we don't take anything
to heaven with us—except our relationships—I found myself
convicted of poor stewardship of not only resources, but of my
relationships too. I mean, I've always known relationships are
most important, but God seemed to highlight it in that moment.
Crazy how that works, isn't it?

We were created by a relational God for interaction with one
another. To have conversations. Go on adventures. Love one
another. My kids always reflect on the times we sat around the
table or vacationed together, not the stuff we've bought for them
over the years.

I believe I've stewarded my relationships with my kids well,
but sometimes I wonder if I could have stopped what I was doing
and made eye contact more often. Should I have taught them
more homemaking skills, even if I dislike cooking and tire easily of

having to repeat instructions multiple times with little or no results? What more could I have done?

Whatever regrets we may harbor at this time of loss need to be dealt with, forgiven, and left in the past so we can move forward into the future. We have many relationships remaining. We have to pull ourselves out of that place of regret and grief and keep putting one foot in front of the other, even if we crawl.

Survival Tip:

How does a mama crawl forward after such a devastating loss?

Focus on your remaining relationships. Don't isolate yourself, no matter how tempting that may be. You can take a day or two or a week here and there. Take a month if you need to. But you must not shut out your significant other, your kids, parents, siblings, friends, or anyone else important in your life. It's important that they know they're loved as much as your deceased children are loved.

Here are a few ideas for maintaining relationships and avoiding isolation in this season of life:

- **While you spend time apart from others, make it time to spend with God.** Don't just binge watch a show or wallow in your emotions. Seek Him and His comfort.
- **Choose a time each day when you will "resurface" for social interaction.** Maybe this is for an hour first thing in the morning while you see everyone off for their day or an hour in the evening for dinner, conversations, and bedtimes.
- **Schedule a family night once per week.** Enjoy a meal with everyone at the table (this will help isolating teenagers as well). Choose to watch a movie as a family or play a game or just have a conversation. The

key is to have everyone participate and make it an entire evening together.

- **Schedule a date night every other week.** This will give you and your husband time alone to process. Maybe you both need a break from grief. Use this time to talk about your hopes, dreams, and future plans.

- **Pick one day a month that you will go out for a meal with a friend.** Use this time to catch up on someone else's life and take the focus off your own. Your friend may ask you how you're doing, of course. If she does, be honest.

A Verse to Focus On:

He who dwells in the secret place of the Most High
Shall abide under the shadow of the Almighty.
I will say of the LORD, "He is my refuge and my fortress;
My God, in Him I will trust."
Psalm 91:1-2

Reflection:

What is something you enjoy doing? Who do you enjoy doing that with? When can you do that this month? Put it on your calendar this week and be sure to keep the date.

CHAPTER 16

forgiveness

Caleb's death isn't the only child loss I've experienced. Between Ezra (my firstborn) and Caleb (my second born), I had two miscarriages. But before I ever married and dreamed of having children with my husband, I had history.

In August of 1994, between my freshman and sophomore year of college, I figured out I'd gotten pregnant when my new clothes started to fit a bit too tightly. When I missed my cycle that month, my boyfriend and I headed off to Wegman's to purchase a pregnancy test that turned out to be positive.

We sat in the stairwell of our dorm and discussed the situation with the conclusion that he didn't want another child at that time. His mother was already raising a child for him while he was away getting his nursing degree. My father had made it very clear in a prior pregnancy scare that I was not to bring a child into this earth out of wedlock, as it would ruin his image in our small-town community, so I wasn't about to tell my parents about my situation. And I was not in a position to raise a child on my own. Against every fiber of my being, we opted for abortion.

Having to make this horrendous decision can stick with you for a very long time. But it doesn't have to follow you into eternity.

When I returned to my dorm room afterward, I called my mother and told her what I'd been through. She cried with me and told me about a new church she and Dad were going to and how she wished I'd told her beforehand. She would have encouraged me to keep the baby—that everything would be all right.

Later that month, Mom shared an article with me from a Focus on the Family magazine entitled "Aaron's Story." At the time I read it, I struggled with forgiveness. Forgiveness for my father, my boyfriend, and the most difficult of all, myself. After reading this article, I begged God to give me a dream of my child, just as the author had. That night, God answered my humble prayer.

I dreamt of my aborted child. I stood in a sandbox on a playground similar to that at my high school. In front of me was a field of the brightest green grass I'd ever seen. The sun shone warmly on the scene, where I was first-person present. I looked down, and at my feet, a toddler played in the sand. She wore pink, corduroy bibs with a white short-sleeved polo shirt with a rounded collar. Her hair was up in pigtails secured with pink marble holders. She stood from her crouched position and stretched her arms toward me, beckoning me to pick her up. As I did, she wrapped her arms tightly around my neck and said, "I love you, Mommy." I responded that I loved her too, and my dream vanished in a wisp.

In that moment, I knew that not only had God forgiven me for my abortion, but my daughter had forgiven me too. That dream set me free from guilt, condemnation, and the need to earn God's love. If He could forgive me of my sin in such a way, I could forgive my father and boyfriend for theirs. And I could forgive myself. When we understand God's forgiveness, it allows us to easily lay down the hurt, offense, bitterness, and animosity we may hold toward another. And it allows room for grace to reside.

Mama, if you've had an abortion or been injured in such a way that it caused you to lose a child, I encourage you to seek the Lord for answers to your tough questions and to ask Him to lead you into the sweet freedom of His forgiveness. You do not have to carry that burden into eternity.

Survival Tip:

Forgiveness may not be a "one and done" event. Sometimes forgiveness happens over the course of moments, days, weeks, months, and years. There have been moments when I've chosen to forgive someone an offense, but the next time he or she commits the same offense, I'm right back where I started with forgiving them. Because it's hard to forget, especially when someone continues to sin against you.

Let's look at what it takes to truly walk in forgiveness of ourselves and others:

1. **Recognition.** First, we have to recognize that someone has caused us harm, whether physically, mentally, emotionally, or spiritually. Have they done it once or is it a repeated offense?
2. **Name it.** What exactly have they done, and how exactly has that made you feel? Be specific. Note it to yourself and be prepared to tell the offender about the offense, if it is physically safe for you to do so. Do not put yourself in further harm's way.
3. **Take it to God.** Tell Him what has happened and how you feel. Vent. Let it out. He can handle your anger, frustration, hurt, attitude, cursing, and all the things much better than any human will be able to do so. I have found that in airing it out with God first, I can see where I may be in the wrong or thinking incorrectly in my heightened emotional state, and I can clearly process what I'm going through. Usually, I'm calm and have found some semblance of peace when I'm finished. Another key is to listen for the Lord's response. And be obedient to it.

4. **Take it to the person who offended you.** Matthew 18:15-17 tells us exactly how to deal with the sin someone has committed against us. First, we take it to that person alone. Remember, *"Love covers all sins"* (Proverbs 10:12b). God doesn't air our dirty laundry in front of multitudes. Neither should we.

5. **If that person refuses to hear you out, take witnesses with you.** Find those who witnessed the offense and bring them with you to speak with the offender. If this doesn't gain you repentance, take it to the church. Call on a pastor to mediate the offense.

6. **Practice forgiveness.** Sometimes I feel an immediate release of the person and the offense when I claim that I forgive them. However, there are many times I must choose forgiveness seven times seventy (that's 490!) times per day. I'm not sure someone could offend me that many times in one day, but what about over years? God calls us to forgive one another so that we may be forgiven of our own sin (Matthew 6:14-15). So, when you don't instantly feel that relief in your heart and spirit, use the power in your tongue to repeat, "Father, I forgive (name them) for (name the offense)," until you do.

A Verse to Focus On:

And you, being dead in your trespasses and the uncircumcision of your flesh, He has made alive together with Him, having forgiven you all trespasses, having wiped out the handwriting of require-ments that was against us, which was contrary to us. And He has taken it out of the way, having nailed it to the cross.
Colossians 2:13-14

Reflection:

Who do you need to forgive? In what way has your child loss stirred up unforgiveness in you? Take that offense and person to the Lord today. Choose forgiveness for yourself and others.

CHAPTER 17

don't fight that healing

Several times throughout the first year after Caleb's death, I had discussions with God regarding the Caleb-sized hole in me that took up room in my heart and gaped wide open every time a thought popped into my head or an external trigger went off. The conversation went like this:

> Me: Lord, I'm not sure you can fill this hole. You're
> not Caleb. And he's the one missing. This hole
> in my heart is Caleb-shaped, not God-shaped.
> This is one hole in my heart You can't fill.
> God: ...
> Me: I mean, really, can you possibly fill it? I know
> You're present in it. But this hole isn't going
> away. Not until I get to come Home and be
> with Caleb again.
> God: ...

I never really got a response from the Lord regarding this Caleb-shaped hole in my heart. Reflecting on it now, a few years down the road, I hear a gentle whisper in my thoughts—that still-small voice the Lord uses to speak to me—saying, "I would never try to fill that Caleb-shaped hole within you. It's reserved for him."

What I learned as I considered that hole is that even though it can't be filled, the rough edges can be smoothed. I just have to allow the s(m)oothing to happen.

God wants to meet us in our pain, our anger, our grief. The question is, do we have the faith to allow Him in?

In John 5:5-6, an invalid is lying next to the Pool of Bethesda. He's been an invalid for thirty-eight years. He wants to get into the water when the angel stirs it, but others beat him to it all the time. Then Jesus comes along and asks this man one question. *"Do you want to be made well?"*

Do we want to allow the Lord to heal us of this grief? This pain? This heartbreak? Or do we want to cling to our grief out of fear of what's to come if we let go ... if we let our child go ... as if we are still able to hold onto him or her in this lifetime? That, Mama, is a choice we each must make before we'll ever be able to live life to the fullest again.

Jesus tells the invalid to *"Get up! Pick up your mat and walk."* The man now had a choice. He could believe that he was well enough to do so, or he could remain an invalid the rest of his days. The Word tells us, *"At once the man was cured; he picked up his mat and walked."* Faith takes action. It takes a determined decision to trust God is faithful and to take that next step forward in life. Notice Jesus didn't tell the man to leave his mat behind. He told him to take it with him.

Survival Tip:

Mama, this is one of the harder things to do in this grief journey. To pick up our mats and walk. To decide that we love and trust God more than we want to cling to our grief ... or our child, if we're being brutally honest. Following the Lord is always going to cost us something. Sometimes it costs us people we love. Unfortunately, that's a reality of life. We all die. Only God knows when. And as unnatural as it is for our babies to beat us Home, God still needs us to live for Him. To do the things He's called us to do for His kingdom so others can experience His love and salvation.

So, it's time for you to admit you have a need. Your heart is broken. You need to be healed.

Next, it's time to desire change. Like the invalid's mat went with him, grief will go with you the rest of your days. But like the invalid who was cured and then walked, you will find that with God at your side, you too will walk. One foot in front of the other. One step at a time.

And as you get farther down that narrow path, you too will notice that the rough edges around that gaping child-shaped hole in your heart have been smoothed out.

And that is how you will get through the rest of your life. It's not easy. But with God it is.

A Verse to Focus On:

But those who wait on the LORD
Shall renew their strength;
They shall mount up with wings like eagles,
They shall run and not be weary,
They shall walk and not faint.
Isaiah 40:31

Reflection:

What losses has the Lord seen you through before? How did you get through them?

pieces of caleb's last night

At nine-something PM, Caleb left his fiancé's birthday party and set off to visit his best friend, who was home from US Army National Guard boot camp on Christmas leave and was scheduled to return January third—the following day.

Only Caleb never made it.

Caleb's fiancé called me when Caleb's friend called her, looking for Caleb.

We know that a resident who lived across the road from Caleb's accident site heard the crash and immediately went out to investigate. When he found our son, he was unresponsive, eyes wide open with a look of surprised shock on his face. The gentleman, the father of one of my niece's (and likely Caleb's) JROTC friends, immediately called 911.

The curve runs alongside a cow pasture. White fencing skirts the edge of the field, keeping the cows inside. At that curve, there is a power pole and a row of large trees, likely oak.

We know Caleb's BMW Z3 spun, slid off the road at the curve where the road is banked, and hit the power pole with the driver's side. It then landed at the bottom of the tree a few feet up the road from the pole. He was facing the opposite direction he was traveling. The driver's side was crumpled inward, and the frame of the car was bent. The power pole was snapped but still standing and would need to be replaced.

surviving the grief journey

the emotional cycle

C aleb,
     Some days it's hard to think beyond the thoughts. Beyond the heartache. Beyond the deep desires to hug you again. Or see your smile. Or watch your eyes light up with joy. Or hear your laughter. Your guitar. Your boots walking across my floor. To be able to just reach out and touch you.

I always told God that you were His first and that no matter what happened, I knew you belonged to Him before you ever belonged to me. That I had the honor, privilege, and blessing to carry, birth, and raise you here to do His will. Even if it meant you made it Home before I did.

And I always considered how David mourned his son and then went back to living his life as God intended. And I thought I could do that too. Keep going after a brief period of mourning.

Boy, was I mistaken. This grief journey is so long and difficult. And I am so much more broken than I ever thought I would be.

Thankfully, God knows ...

I was talking with Miss Shawnna this morning, and we were commenting on how our hearts just seem to know when it's "that time of the month." Like we have an internal alarm that goes off and we begin to leak tears. Every month. Like clockwork.

SURVIVING THE YEAR OF FIRSTS

As your dad went back to work this Monday, he mentioned how sad I seemed. How regular it seemed.

I don't know what it is about this seventh month. How it feels worse than the fourth month. Or the sixth month. How I long to find His strength in my weakness. His peace that passes all understanding in the chaos of my emotional turmoil and the storm in my heart. His comfort in my distress.

And how some days it just feels so out of reach. Just. Like. You.

And so I leak. Big soggy tears. None wasted. All stored in God's bottle. And I try to look at the brighter side of the story. And picture you living your eternal life with Him.

Mama, did you know that grief tears are special? Different from other tears we cry?

We have three types of tears: basal, reflex, and psychic (or emotional). Basal tears are the natural coating in our eyes that keep them healthy. Reflex tears are those that surface when we cut an onion, get something in our eye, or have an allergic reaction. These flush the bad irritants from our eyes.

And then there are the psychic, or emotional, tears we cry. These are the tears that flood our eyes in response to things that bring us joy, grief, or rage. These tears contain protein-based stress hormones. Emotional tears also contain more manganese, which is a mood stabilizer. These tears contain natural painkillers.[1]

So, Mama, when you can't control the urge to release that grief, ugly cry your heart out. The tears you shed will be healing you as you cry.

Check out this article from the Smithsonian, which shares photographs of different types of tears that were taken by artist Rose-Lynn Fisher:

https://www.smithsonianmag.com/science-nature/the-micro scopic-structures-of-dried-human-tears-180947766/

Survival Tip:

Find a friend to walk through this season of grief alongside you. Someone who isn't your spouse or child or parent. Maybe she's your best friend. Maybe she isn't. Maybe she'll become a treasured friend in the process.

You need someone who understands what you're going through. Maybe someone who has lost a child herself. Maybe someone, like Shawnna, who was like a mama to your child.

This person should be someone who will get it when you call her and say, "It's that time of the month again."

Make it a point to have lunch or dinner or coffee/tea once a month. It will be healthy to have that connection and that steadiness in your life for the next year and beyond.

A Verse to Focus On:

Those who sow in tears
Shall reap in joy.
He who continually goes forth weeping,
Bearing seed for sowing,
Shall doubtless come again with rejoicing,
Bringing his sheaves with him.
Psalm 126:5-6

Reflection:

What was the last thing that triggered big, soggy, ugly cry, sobbing tears? Try writing a letter to your child about it.

CHAPTER 19

denial

Mama, it's okay to experience all the stages of grief (Denial, Anger, Bargaining, Depression, and Acceptance). They may come in order. They may not. You may experience none of them, some of them, or all of them. How they show up will be different for everyone.

I'm a huge fan of crime shows. *NCIS. Bones. CSI. Criminal Minds. Longmire. Chicago PD. Blue Bloods. Elsbeth.* I also read a lot of romantic suspense and thrillers. Combine that with Caleb's desire to serve his country as a Marine and making it partially through boot camp before a medical discharge, and you can imagine where my brain went when I entered the denial stage of grief. This stage came about a month into my grieving process.

Curiously, Caleb's car keys and phone were never recovered from the crash site. His phone may have ended up jammed somewhere in the wreckage of the car. But to have his keys entirely disappear is ... odd. The tow company didn't get them, they weren't in his belongings at the hospital, and the first responders didn't seem to know where they were. I still wonder if the man who called 911 pulled them from the ignition. Maybe they ended up in the wreckage because someone dropped them, and they were swept away with the debris. Who knows?

Also, we never were asked to identify him, nor did we get the opportunity to say goodbye that night. They took him from the operating room to the morgue. We didn't have that closure experience until the funeral home presented his body for our private family viewing.

When I went into denial, my writer brain took off. For about a month, I imagined the government really wanted him for a skill they recognized at boot camp and had done one of those body-swap moves. I thought it would be cool if, one day, he strolled up to our front door and told us he'd been on a classified mission for a season, and due to the nature of it, no one could know he was still alive.

Hey, it brought me the peace my brain needed for a short season. Please don't judge.

In an article on VeryWellMind.com, Sanjana Gupta writes, "Denial is a defense mechanism that helps minimize the pain of the loss. It's your brain's way of protecting you from the pain, so you have some time to adjust to your new reality. Denial is typically experienced immediately after a loss, as your brain works to process it."[1]

Note that denial helps to minimize the pain and protect you from further harm. So, when your brain wants to shut down and block things out or takes you to some crazy story world, don't panic. It's all part of the process. Just don't get stuck there. Get help if you don't start to move out of that alternate reality on your own.

As I write this, God reminds me that Caleb is off on a mission —a heavenly mission. He is serving the Lord in new ways with new purposes. Much higher purposes than he had here on Earth. And in that, I can find peace and joy.

Survival Tip:

Denial is the action of declaring something untrue. Your

brain may try to tell you that you didn't just lose a loved one, a part of you, a child. You may cry out and ask where your child is.

The tip here is simple:

- **Let it happen.**
- **Ask the questions.**
- **Say it isn't so.**

Give your mind time to process what has happened as a protection mechanism for your heart.

A Verse to Focus On:

My soul still remembers
And sinks within me.
This I recall to my mind,
Therefore I have hope.
Through the LORD's mercies we are not consumed,
Because His compassions fail not.
Lamentations 3:20-22

Reflection:

What does your denial stage look like? What have you taken from it?

CHAPTER 20

foggy

You've likely noticed by now that grief comes in waves. Some days will be okay. On others, grief will start afar off the horizon and slowly roll in until it crashes against your soul. Some days are sunny, while others fill with clouds and fog.

Grief fog.

You may discover you can't focus. That simple tasks you could do on autopilot are no longer simple. You forget things easily and have a difficult time remembering names of people or pets you've known forever. You may find yourself rereading that sentence multiple times before you can process what you've read. You're lucky if it sinks in. Have you forgotten to pay the bills?

Mama, your brain is focused on your loss. It's trying to make sense of what has happened, to process the trauma and the stress you've suffered. Your brain is in survival mode. Neurologist Lisa M. Shulman, MD, FAAN explains, "Over the long term, grief can disrupt the diverse cognitive domains of memory, decision-making, visuospatial function, attention, word fluency, and the speed of information processing."[1]

So, when you're a word person who is trying desperately to come up with that word mid-sentence—that one you've used since you learned it in that eight-grade English class vocabulary lesson—and it just won't roll to the tip of your tongue, remember: it's not you. It's grief brain.

Survival Tip:

You can help yourself by writing things down.

- **Keep a notebook nearby.** Jot down appointment dates and times, grocery lists, to-do lists, etc.
- **Use a monthly calendar to track your bills.** Or, put them all—at least the important ones like mortgage, electric, heating fuel, water, and trash removal—on autopay.
- **Journal your thoughts and emotions.** This helps to process what you're going through.
- **Talk it out.** I find that talking through things out loud also helps me process all those thoughts running through my mind and the emotions that come with them. Talk to yourself. Talk to God. Call a friend and have lunch. Talk with your counselor or therapist, pastor, or trusted confidant.

Whatever you do, don't keep your grief locked inside. Your body and brain need to work it out and return to some semblance of normal—even if that normal is new.

A Verse to Focus On:

You will keep him in perfect peace,
Whose mind is stayed on You.
Isaiah 26:3

Reflection:

What is something you now struggle with that you never had an issue with in the past? What can you do to help yourself overcome that struggle?

CHAPTER 21

Longing for heaven

Mama, it is perfectly normal in grieving to feel you no longer wish to be here. Because your child is gone, you long for what comes next. You want to know what it's like to have no more sorrow, to not fear which loved one will die next, to spend a day wrapped in joy rather than crying. These feelings are perfectly normal in this season of life, and you're not alone in thinking about eternal life.

I have a deep longing not only to see Caleb again, but to see Jesus as Caleb is seeing Him now. It's a strong pull in my heart. One that brings a knot to my throat. A tightness in my chest. A deep desire that isn't satisfied.

I just want to be wrapped in the Father's love on a whole other level than we experience of Him while we are still on this earth. I want to be in heaven, where there's no more pain, death, sorrow, or crying. I'm so done with all of this.

My mom tells me I've had this longing since before Caleb passed. I don't remember, but if that's true, that longing is magnified now that my son is gone.

Ecclesiastes caught my attention on a new level. It's that vanity of vanities that I found myself questioning. What's the point of all we do here if it just leads to death? Why did I have

Caleb in the first place, just to have him taken out of my reach at nineteen? "What was the point, Lord?" I cried numerous times. *Is it all in vain?*

All the while, God patiently waited for me to accept that I am still earthbound. Once I did, He reminded me that He still has plans for me in this lifetime. And it was He who placed that longing in me, so that I would come to Him with everything I have in me. It's relationship that I desire more than anything on this earth. Relationship with my Father, who loves me.

Survival Tip:

Take a moment to sit in a quiet place today. Consider what your child may be doing in this moment.

For example, I can see Caleb in his cowboy boots and hat, guitar in his hands, standing before the Lord, playing Him the song he just wrote. I can see the smile on God's face as He listens to Caleb's composition for the King. The Father's brilliance shines on Caleb's face like the glow of the golden hour here on earth, magnified. I hear God compliment him, "Well done ..." and watch as Caleb turns to wander off to a distant field filled with animals to enjoy.

Consider Philippians 4:8 as you do this activity.

> Finally, brethren, whatever things are true, what-
> ever things are noble, whatever things are just,
> whatever things are pure, whatever things are
> lovely, whatever things are of good report, if
> there is any virtue and if there is anything
> praiseworthy—meditate on these things. The
> things which you learned and received and
> heard and saw in me, these do, and the God of
> peace will be with you.

Think on these things. Spend that moment with your child,

even if it's only in your imagination. Shift your focus to eternal life, rather than earthly death. Stay there awhile. Whisper the things you wish you could tell your child in person. It's healing to release those words, and maybe the Lord will whisper back with a glimpse of heaven.

You could also read *Imagine Heaven* by John Burke. This book gave me a lot of hope, inspiration, and anticipation as I read about others' near-death experiences and the glimpses of heaven they shared. There are some passages that may be difficult to read due to your grief, but they are worth reading.

Finally, allow God to help you make peace with surviving your child. Let him lighten the guilt load you may carry. And take your time in this process with Him. You're not on anyone else's schedule. And He is patient.

A Verse to Focus On:

How lovely is Your tabernacle,
O LORD of hosts!
My soul longs, yes, even faints
For the courts of the LORD;
My heart and my flesh cry out for the living God.
Psalm 84:1-2

Reflection:

What is one thing you imagine for your child in eternity? How does that encourage you to trust God with your life on earth?

amnesia

Mama, sometimes grief can be scary.

When we went on our first family vacation after Caleb's passing, I expected to miss him and experience a trigger or two. What happened truly frightened me.

The first night at the campsite, we sat around a fire and enjoyed the peacefulness. A few young adults cruised the campground on a golf cart, playing country music through their karaoke speaker. On one trip past us, Hank Williams Jr. was on. The song was "Country Boys Can Survive." There's a line in that song about how his New York friend calls him "Hillbilly." It's the line Caleb's friend used to nickname him. In that moment, I smiled and felt the joy of knowing he is in our hearts. I considered it a touch from heaven.

I went to bed happy, expecting sweet sleep our first night away.

In the middle of the night, I woke up nauseous with acid reflux issues. The physical discomfort was quickly overridden by my sudden onset of grief amnesia (yes, there is such a thing). I knew Caleb was gone and that we had a grave site. But I *could not* recall any other information. I knew he had died but couldn't remember how or when or why.

This experience was like reliving Caleb's death all over again. Like getting the call from the hospital and not knowing if he would survive or not. Like sitting in the surgery lobby waiting for the doctor to come out and pronounce him dead. Like the instant, gut-wrenching, heart-stopping moment all over again.

I sat in the bathroom of our little cabin with my upset stomach, sobbing for twenty minutes as quietly as I could—so I wouldn't awaken and upset my children and husband—crying out to God in prayer while wracking my brain trying to remember what had happened and why I'd buried my son.

S-C-A-R-E-D out of my mind.

Because that is just not normal.

And I knew I knew the details. But I couldn't recall them. At all.

Finally, they started to emerge. Like flashes of scenes. The energy pole with the flags taped to it on the bend of a country road. The hospital. The family gathered at our kitchen table. The friends talking about Caleb at the Celebration of Life. The graveside ceremony.

As my tears kept rolling, I asked God to please, please, please bring me comfort. And a verse. I needed a verse.

> Yea, though I walk through the valley of the
>   shadow of death,
> I will fear no evil;
> For You are with me;
> Your rod and Your staff,
> they comfort me.
> *Psalm 23:4*

That's where God took me in that moment. As I read the words, peace flooded from my head to my toes.

Vic had woken as I moved from the bathroom to crawl back into bed and retrieved my phone to look up this verse. Although he asked what had happened, I didn't explain much. Just that I missed our son. I cried myself back to sleep in my husband's comforting embrace.

There were a few more moments when grief overwhelmed me throughout our vacation. I shed some tears over an elk burger a couple of evenings later. But nothing in this journey of experiences has come close to the grief amnesia in how deeply traumatizing it was.

Thankfully, Hope prevails. And Love continues to overcome even the darkest nights.

Survival Tip:

Sometimes we pray for God to show us where we left something, like our keys. Thankfully, God knows exactly where those things can be found. He can do the same with our memories.

In those times when you feel like you can't remember a detail about your child, his or her life, their passing, or any other thing, ask God to quicken the memory for your recall. It may take a few minutes for them to return, as it did for mine. But God is faithful.

And if, for some reason, He doesn't, maybe it's because He knows you need to forget that one thing so you can move on in your healing. And that's okay too.

A Verse to Focus On:

Shall Your lovingkindness be declared in the grave?
Or Your faithfulness in the place of destruction?
Shall Your wonders be known in the dark?
And Your righteousness in the land of forgetfulness?
But to You I have cried out, O LORD,
And in the morning my prayer comes before You.
Psalm 88:11-13

Reflection:

What's a scripture verse or quote that has brought you comfort in your grief? Why did it touch you in that particular moment?

CHAPTER 23

dreams

Mama, I know you long to see your child again. To talk with him or her. To connect one more time. If you haven't had a dream of your child since their passing, I pray you do.

There is a special term for these types of dreams. Dr. Joshua Black had a dream about his deceased father that affected him so profoundly, he pursued a Ph.D. in such dreams. He calls them "grief dreams." These dreams can be positive or negative, can feature the deceased or not, and typically hold healing power for the griever. Interestingly, grief dreams tend to be more vivid and feel different than an average dream.[1]

I can attest to Dr. Black's findings. My daughter, Hannah, had been having dreams of Caleb on a regular basis, and I was a tad jealous of this until I had one of my own. The following is the first dream I had of my son, which came months after he'd passed.

Hannah, Dad, and I were driving past a school and decided to surprise you.

We were walking the hallway and came to a door with a window making up the top half. We could see in. I stood next to Dad with a younger Hannah in front of me, my arms crossed over her chest in a hug.

The room you were in was big, like a gymnasium or cafeteria. The teacher's desk was at the front with the door behind it. The students' desks were single, in rows, like you were taking the SATs or another big test.

The female teacher called you up to her desk.

You stood tall in your JROTC uniform, made eye contact with me, smiled, and waved.

I was waving back at you as you walked toward us when ...

My husband woke me and told me to let the dog out because Blaize was whining outside our bedroom door at one o'clock in the morning, interrupting my very first dream of Caleb since his death.

To say I was upset is a huge understatement. I was disappointed. Frustrated. Sad. And angry. All at the same time. Stupid dog!

This dream brought me great joy in the midst of my grief. I saw the light in my son's eyes, the smile on his face (an expression of his excitement to see us), and his desire to interact after what seemed a lifetime apart.

Survival Tip:

Keep a dream journal next to your bed. When you dream of your child, whether positively or negatively, write it down. Consider the following:

- **What happened in the dream?**
- **Was it positive or negative?**

- **How did you feel when you woke up?**
- **What in your dream, if anything, reflected your emotions?** Dr. Black shared an example of something falling on you as representing the crushing grief you feel regarding the death of your child.

A Verse to Focus On:

When I remember You on my bed,
I meditate on You in the night watches.
Because You have been my help,
Therefore in the shadow of Your wings I will rejoice.
My soul follows close behind You;
Your right hand upholds me.
Psalm 63:6-8

Reflection:

Write down a dream your child had for their life that was never fulfilled. Is there anything you can do to bring even a part of that dream to life in honor of your child?

CHAPTER 24

part of me

M ama, well-meaning friends and family members may tell
you that you've grieved long enough, and you should (or
need to) move on. It's time to get back to living. While there will
come a time when your grief doesn't knock you on your butt each
time it pops up, it's not up to them to tell you when you're ready
to let go of grief's hand and move forward on your own. Especially if they've never experienced child loss.

While our friends and family members may not understand
what we're going through, God understands the heartbreak of
losing a child. Our Father in heaven sent His only begotten Son to
us so we could be saved from our sin and spend eternity in relationship with Him (John 3:16). For three long days, He suffered
the grief of child loss. He understands our grief on a level no
human possibly could.

And He gifted us mamas with something super special that
scientists have only recently discovered. Like a secret treasure.
Mama, did you know that your child leaves some of his or her
DNA and fetal cells in you when you are pregnant? It's called
fetal microchimerism.

Several researchers have discovered Y sex (male) chromosomes
in mothers decades after they've given birth. These Y chromo-

somes are passed from father to son, so the only explanation is that the son is passing them to his mother as he develops in her womb.

Because girls' chromosomes are similar to their mother's, it's difficult to say whether or not she is passing them on to her mama, but it makes sense that this could also be possible.

Fetal microchimerism is still being researched, but there is evidence these cells can be found in many of the mother's organ tissues and tend to travel toward cancers, tumors, rheumatoid arthritis, and other diseases. They're still figuring out whether the cells are helping or hindering a mother's health.

Based on my faith in God and knowing how intricately He created us, I'd guess they're helping more than hindering. And I believe those cells will help heal our broken hearts.

There's some comfort in knowing I still carry a piece of Caleb within me. I would imagine you would feel the same knowing you still carry part of your child within you.

So, when your heart is breaking in two, remember that your child is still with you, and God knows exactly how you feel in this moment. He *will* heal your broken heart. Rest in knowing this.

Survival Tip:

First, remember to treat others the way you would want them to treat you. When others try to tell you what your grieving process should look like, politely explain that you will grieve for as long and as hard as you need to find healing.

Second, print a wallet-sized photo of your child. Use an index card or a piece of cardstock, along with that photo, to create a memory of your child. You could also include a small token—like the guitar pick I have in my wallet—or add a quote or verse that reminds you of your child. Decorate the memory however you'd like.

When you're finished, place your creation in your wallet, purse, or someplace you can take it with you. You'll have a token of your child to carry wherever you go. When you miss him or her so much your heart aches, you can pull out the memory and cherish it in the moment.

A Verse to Focus On:

"For the LORD will not cast off forever.
Though He causes grief,
Yet He will show compassion
According to the multitudes of His mercies."
Lamentations 3:31-32

Reflection:

What's one of the last things your child did with or for you?

the bunny

Caleb and his fiancé had gone to Build-A-Bear and created a bunny and a monkey for each other. The best part of these stuffed animals was that they had a voice recording tucked inside of them. Caleb had always told me he'd left a silly message for her, but he'd never said what it was.

One particularly tearful day in March, I stopped by to see Caleb's fiancé's mama, Shawnna. I just needed to feel close to him and seeing her and her daughter always helped.

After talking to Shawnna for a bit, I ventured upstairs to see her daughter. I asked her if I could listen to the message Caleb had left in Bunny. To my surprise, she willingly let go of Bunny long enough for me to have a moment.

I wasn't expecting what I heard when I pushed that button in Bunny's paw.

"I forgot what I was gonna say ... oh ... oh yeah ... *I love you.*"

I. LOVE. YOU.

What Caleb's fiancé and her mama didn't know is that for the past month, I had been longing to hear Caleb say, "I love you, Mama."

It's the last thing he ever said to me.

And it's what I needed to hear again.

Later that evening, she allowed her parents to record Bunny's words so I could listen to Caleb say "I love you" anytime I need to.

Her allowing me to listen to Bunny made room for God to touch my heart on a deep, deep level. I'll always treasure that moment.

surviving triggers

CHAPTER 25

daily Triggers

Mama, every sense we have—sight, smell, taste, sound, and touch—leaves us open to an intense emotional reaction when we are suddenly reminded of our child (or another loved one) who has died. These responses are called grief triggers. Triggers come in all shapes and sizes and can strike in any place at any time.

I'll never forget the first time I was driving and came across a Roebuck Landscaping Truck. Every time I used to pass one, I would strain to see if Caleb was driving. No longer could I look for him in a truck. And that wrecked me. Do you know how difficult it is to drive when you can't see through the giant messy tears you're shedding?

But God can also use the triggers to heal our broken hearts. A few months after Caleb's death, Gideon, his younger brother, alerted me to Caleb's Spotify playlists. While Caleb's country music and guitar lick lists were much longer, his worship playlist was a reflection of his recent return to a deeper relationship with the Lord. The songs he'd chosen for this particular list gave me a glimpse into my son's heart for God. This was yet another touch of healing for my heart that came straight from my Father.

While every trigger can grab your heart and rip it out of your chest again and again, God can also use those triggers to bring healing. Your quest is to look for the blessing in the pain.

Survival Tip:

Mama, for the first year and probably longer, expect to be triggered on a daily basis. Several of those triggers may surprise you at first, but after a short while, you should be able to anticipate them.

When you find yourself triggered, try the following:

- **Take note of what the trigger was.** Was it a date? A scent? Driving past the cemetery? Hearing someone say "Mama" just like your son would? Make a mental note or write it down.
- **Acknowledge the emotion you're feeling.** Are you angry? Sad? Do you want to run and hide? Fight? While you acknowledge the emotion, note your response to it.
- **Allow yourself time to grieve.** The trigger can last for a brief moment, or it can lay you out for the day. It shouldn't last longer than several hours, though. If it does, it may be time to seek help from a grief counselor.
- **Take a few deep breaths and ask God to comfort you.** These can help calm your reaction to the trigger.
- **Let the memories come.** Try to focus on positive memories. What part of this trigger is associated with that memory? If the memories are negative, try to replace them with a positive memory. Again, focus on life, not death. Even if it's cradling your child in your arms as an infant—long before his or her life spiraled out of control.

A Verse to Focus On:

He heals the brokenhearted
And binds up their wounds.
Psalm 147:3

Reflection:

What's a favorite memory of your child that surfaces when your grief is triggered?

memories

Facebook keeps pulling up memories from the past year, and it's bittersweet to see my boy's smile, the light in his eyes, to reminisce on the life he lived.

With the memories, all the emotions we mamas experience while raising our kids flood in. The joy of holding a newborn. The frustrations of toddlerhood and exploration of boundaries. The weariness and sleepless nights. The pride of watching them hit milestones. The stress of temper tantrums and sibling rivalries. The drama of teenagers. The fear that something may go wrong before they have a chance to live.

Some days it seems surreal. I find myself wondering if I was just living a dream. Was he really here for nineteen years? Did I give birth and watch him grow? Was it only a few months ago I last hugged him goodbye, not realizing it would be our final goodbye on earth? Sometimes it feels like he was never here, while other times it's as if he was just here yesterday. Such a strange thing, this grief.

It's in these moments that I hear God reminding me that yes, Caleb really was here. Being his mom is one of the most important and best things I got to do in this life. Even when I've struggled, doubted myself and my abilities as a mother, or felt unimportant, I was blessed and honored to give birth to, raise, and love my son. For nineteen years and two months, he was mine.

So, as much as social media can be frustrating, I've learned to appreciate the value in it. Between my Facebook feed, others' posts, and even my son's posts, social media has been like having a scrapbook album I can scroll through, preserving my memories. Some things I've held near and dear for years, and others I'd forgotten. Although bittersweet, I'm thankful I have the ability to go there.

Mama, as much as you think you're going to forget your child, you won't. You may forget certain details of events and conversations. *But you will never forget your child.* Rest today in knowing that.

Survival Tip:

Here are a few things you can do as the days pass and you find yourself feeling like those memories may be slipping away:

- **Create a scrapbook of your son or daughter.** This may not be the time to attempt catching up on scrapbooks of their childhood you never had the time to finish before. Instead, pull the highlights of his or her life, from birth through their death, and compile them into one album. Write down the memories of those moments so they don't fade over time.
- **Create a notebook of memories of your child.** Write down your memories and have your family and your child's friends write theirs. I recommend doing it sooner than later, as we forget some of the details over time.
- **Find your kid's social media accounts.** Scroll Facebook, Instagram, Snapchat, TikTok, and YouTube, and take the time to reminisce. Remember

the light in your child's eyes or the pouty lip. Listen to his voice in his videos or in the written words of her posts. You can screenshot posts and save them in a file, as well.

Relive the moments and take comfort in knowing they truly were a part of your life, even if it only seemed to be for a moment in time.

A Verse to Focus On:

"Can a woman forget her nursing child,
And not have compassion on the son of her womb?
Surely they may forget,
Yet I will not forget you.
See, I have inscribed you on the palms of My hands."
Isaiah 49:15-16a

Reflection:

What's your fondest memory of your child? If a flood of them come to mind, that's okay. Write them all down.

CHAPTER 27

shopping Triggers

T he girls and I were in Walmart getting some things, and I grabbed a box of donuts for my youngest son. As I left the bakery section, I saw some lemon bite desserts. My mind said, "Caleb would like those," and the sudden squeeze of my heart reminded me he wasn't here to give them to, welling tears in my eyes.

No more lemon-filled Krispy Kremes. Ramen Bowls. Chicken Nuggets. Oranges. And so many other things he loved.

Mama, when you're walking down the aisle at Walmart or Target and your heart jolts as you pass something you would have bought your child, don't worry one bit about whether someone else will notice your tears. Take a break and go to your car if you need to. Or, let the tears fall as you push your buggy past the items and continue shopping for your family's needs.

We belong to the club none of us want to belong to, but it's incredibly comforting to know there are others who understand why we're crying at the store.

Survival Tip:

Just because they're gone doesn't mean we have to stop

buying things they would enjoy. Go ahead and get it. Here are some ideas what you could do:

- **Cook his or her favorite meal for family dinner.** Talk about your favorite times with your child while your family enjoys their favorite meal together.

I take our kids to Bojangles for the Chicken Supreme meals (chicken tenders, fries, and drink). We've stopped calling them Bo Boxes and started calling them Caleb Boxes. He used to drive through with his brother or sister and park and talk with them. It's special. We haven't stopped because he's gone. Sometimes, you just need a Caleb Box.

- **Gift the item you purchase.** Which of his or her friends or family member would appreciate the gesture?
- **Take it home and put it on a shelf.** Smile at the memory every time you walk past it.
- **Take it to the gravesite.** Leave it there for a season. I bought a Rocky Balboa pencil sharpener when I was passing through the airport in Philadelphia because Caleb was a fan of the Rocky movies. Rocky is standing with his arms in the air, celebrating a training success. I imagine Caleb standing in the same stance, celebrating his victory over death and new life in heaven. The metal pencil sharpener has been at his gravesite since I returned from that trip.

A Verse to Focus On:

Rejoice with those who rejoice, and weep with those who weep.
Romans 12:15

Reflection:

What was your child's favorite meal, character, activity, etc.? Make
a list today.

CHAPTER 28

unexpected triggers

Mama, God knows our pain. As a Father, He has grieved the death of His Son. As the One who searches our hearts, He knows exactly what we feel and how deep that wound goes.

One of my favorite Sunday mornings at church has always been Baby Dedication Sunday. This is the Sunday where mamas and daddies bring their infant- to toddler-aged children onstage to declare they will raise them in such a way that the kids will come to know Jesus as their Lord and Savior. The pastor will say a few words before proceeding to pray for the families and their wee ones. It's such a tender moment when you're in it. One that I've cherished four times over.

It is also a very serious moment in motherhood. One where you realize that this child is not yours first—he or she is God's first. Which means you have to trust Him with this child. Regardless of what may come.

Throughout my years of raising my children, I had conversations with God that went something like, "I know they're Yours first, that You've loaned them to me, so if You ever decide You need them back, I'm okay with that. I will be okay with that."

That doesn't mean I never struggled with doubt or worry or

wondered if I would crumble if God did take one of them Home before me. Although the pain of Caleb's death still wrings my heart until my eyes water, I'm not angry with God for calling him Home. I trust my Father above all.

When I walked into church that first baby dedication Sunday after Caleb's death, and the mamas and daddies with all their babies climbed the steps onto that stage, I faced an unexpected trigger. *I know the cost of dedicating my babies to the Lord.*

God knows the cost intimately. He knew when Mary conceived baby Jesus through the seed of the Holy Spirit that one day He would turn His head while His only begotten Son hung on a cross so that Caleb and the rest of us who believe in Him could spend eternity with Him.

God knows how to bind that wound in such a way that we can bear it until it's our turn to go Home. He also gives us the strength to carry on as we continue raising our remaining children.

Survival Tip:

Mama, rather than run from the pain, I encourage you to find the strength to endure it. Allow yourself the opportunity for God to sit in the fire with you. For Jesus to wake up in the boat. For Holy Spirit to overwhelm you with His comfort.

- **Take note of when you're going to be confronted with triggers.** Baby dedications are usually announced ahead of time. You know when you'll be around children, such as being scheduled in nursery or children's church, heading back to a teaching job or nursing or social work, taking care of a sibling's or neighbor's kids, etc. The impact of a trigger is lessened a smidgeon when we acknowledge we are going to be facing when we round that corner.
- **Carry tissues in your purse.**

- **Let anyone in management or administrative positions know you're grieving.** Alert them to the fact that you may need to excuse yourself for brief moments as you process the tears, anger, or jealousy. Ask them to be prepared to send someone to cover you in those moments.
- **Make the call to excuse yourself when you need to.** Take the day off to care for yourself.
- **Allow the grief to process, rather than holding it all inside.** Remember that what isn't dealt with internally will eventually express itself externally. And not in a good way.
- **Have an answer for anyone who asks if you're okay or what's wrong.** Be truthful. Talk about your grief and share your heart. Prepare a kind response for those who may say something insensitive.

A Verse to Focus On:

Even in laughter the heart may sorrow,
And the end of mirth may be grief.
Proverbs 14:13

Reflection:

What triggers have surprised you? How can you manage them by being proactive with a plan?

CHAPTER 29

relational triggers

M ama, sometimes you will face someone's grief, and it will look like blame or offense. These are difficult enough when you're grieving the loss of your child, but it's even more difficult to face when it's a family member or close friend expressing their grief in these ways with you or your family as the recipient.

Sometimes people don't know how to express their grief, so they resort to finding a way to be offended. Or they need to release their anger but don't know how, so they blame the parents for the death of the child. Even a spouse, mom, dad, or a sibling can be the one who doesn't know how to manage grief and place blame on someone close to them.

This sounds entirely unfair. It is. But it happens.

Here's what we need to keep in mind: they lost a loved one too. It's in this season that our family and friends need grace. Grace to grieve. Grace to get over the mountain of grief. Grace to heal.

When we can come to an understanding that blame and offense are misplaced grief, we can more easily bear the load of it. Especially when we recognize it's not our load to bear, but Jesus'.

Survival Tip:

When someone else tries to put their grief on you through blame or offense:

- **Acknowledge your child's death is not your fault.**
- **Give the person the space he or she needs to process their own grief.**
- **Leave your arms and your door open** for the day they recover from their loss and allow opportunity for your relationship to be restored and renewed.
- **Until then, find a way to keep up with him or her via someone close and trusted.** Ask about your friend or family member. Check their social media accounts. And let someone close to him or her know you still care about them.
- **Operate in forgiveness.** They know not what they do when blinded by grief.
- **Lift them in prayer.** Ask God to heal their hearts and bring peace in the process.

A Verse to Focus On:

Let no corrupt word proceed out of your mouth, but what is good for necessary edification, that it may impart grace to the hearers. And do not grieve the Holy Spirit of God, by whom you were sealed for the day of redemption. Let all bitterness, wrath, anger, clamor, and evil speaking be put away from you, with all malice. And be kind to one another, tenderhearted, forgiving one another, even as God in Christ forgave you.
Ephesians 4:29-32

Reflection:

How have you been hurt by someone else's words or actions during your grieving process? Write what you would say to that person if you could offer them forgiveness in person.

CHAPTER 30

Location, location, location

L ocations can be as much a trigger as any sight, sound, taste, texture, or scent.

My son was taken to a local hospital, where he died on a surgery table. The first time I had a need to go to the emergency room, I spent the entire drive praying for peace while anticipating an emotional breakdown upon arrival. I dreaded being there. My father was the patient this time, and although things turned out okay for him, my spirit was a little crushed having to be at the location attached to my son's death.

My daughter struggled with attending church, because we'd chosen to have the Celebration of Life there instead of at a funeral home. Church is where life happens, and Vic and I wanted to celebrate Caleb's life. Plus, I've had enough of funeral homes in my life. I didn't want to sit or stand in one for hours again. What I hadn't realized was how much this decision would affect our surviving children. For the next two years, all Hannah could see on Sunday mornings was the casket in front of the stage. She stopped coming into the sanctuary and listened to service in the café, if she attended church at all.

Another day, I was spending time with my friends. We'd been out taking pictures. As we drove back from lunch, we passed a

Roebuck Landscaping truck, the local skate park where Caleb broke his wrist trying out the bowl, and the hospital again. I silently cried most of the way home, my emotional flood similar to the night he died.

Expect there to be triggers that remind you of your son or daughter, the life they lived, and their passing wherever you go.

Survival Tip:

Mama, you cannot stay home forever. Eventually you will need to go somewhere, do something, and live life outside your home. Here are a few things you can do in preparation for locational triggers:

- **List three to five locations you can expect to be triggered.** I have found that if I can't avoid a location and mentally prepare myself for the inevitable, I don't trigger as easily, if at all. I focus on a positive memory and my love for my son, and I find I can endure the time in that place.
- **Try to avoid that location by taking a different route**. Or you could send someone in your stead or choose not to go at all.
- **Focus on why you're there in this moment if the location is unavoidable.** My youngest son had a marching band competition at a particular school. I didn't realize until I was walking across the parking lot that this was the same school where, several years prior, I'd watched Caleb compete in a JROTC drill competition. It triggered me, and for a brief moment I shed a few tears. That drill competition was a great experience and is a fond memory of my son. I focused on that to stop the tears. Then, I focused on Gideon's marching band competition and enjoyed the day

without further emotional distress. Be in the moment, Mama.

A Verse to Focus On:

"Let not your heart be troubled; you believe in God, believe also in Me. In My Father's house are many mansions; if it were not so, I would have told you. I go to prepare a place for you. And if I go and prepare a place for you, I will come again and receive you to Myself; that where I am, there you may be also. And where I go you know, and the way you know."
John 14:1-4

Reflection:

The Word reminds us that Jesus went to prepare a place for believers. What do you think your child's mansion in his or her Father's house looks like?

CHAPTER 31

your child is more than a statistic

In January 2023, I joined an online challenge that involved going through the book of Proverbs and included a three-day Kingdom Wealth Workshop. When the speaker talked about protecting ourselves from major accidents, guess which year he chose to provide statistics from regarding vehicle accidents? 2021. The year Caleb died in a single-car accident. Can you say *triggered*?

In 2021, there were an estimated 6,106,367 police-reported motor vehicle accidents across the United States.[1] Of those, 147,724 were in South Carolina[2]. Nationally, 42,939 involved fatalities. 1,112 of them were in South Carolina, and 1,198 people died in these, my son being one of them.

This isn't the first time this statistic has triggered me. South Carolina posts traffic fatality statistics on variable message signs over our highways. We have at least one in our area, where I did not enjoy seeing my son's statistic announced every time I drove under it. The first time, I choked up. Afterward, it annoyed me more than anything else.

What I want you to know, Mama, is that your child is far more than a mere statistic. Whether he or she was a cancer patient, died from SIDS, overdosed, committed suicide, was murdered, died in a car accident, or any other form of death that could be counted as a statistic, that is not the most important facet of who your child was. *Is.*

The Creator of the universe molded and formed your child in your womb—or the womb of the mama who birthed him or her, if he or she was adopted or birthed by surrogate. He or she was perfectly and wonderfully made in God's image and likeness and loved beyond what we can begin to imagine or think. That, Mama, is the most important facet of who your child is.

Survival Tip:

When I consider Caleb's accident—because those thoughts still surface from time to time and probably always will—I wonder if he would have survived had there been a guard rail at the curve. Word has it that curve is dangerous and multiple accidents have occurred there. So, when a recent survey came out regarding traffic safety in our area, I made sure to suggest they add a guardrail to that portion of the road.

Mama, if your child's tragic death keeps you awake at night and finds you asking, "What if?" on a regular basis or leaves you longing for a different outcome for other children and their mamas than what you've experienced, consider getting creative and helping others.

Find a local, regional, or national organization you can serve that is fighting the injustices centered around your child's death. Pour your resources, time, and creativity into supporting positive change in our world. Some of you may even want to start your own organization. Ask God to lead you into His perfect will.

A Verse to Focus On:

Before I formed you in the womb I knew you;
Before you were born I sanctified you...
Jeremiah 1:5

Reflection:

What are five character traits you loved about your child? How did he or she reflect God's image in his or her life?

close to heaven

P lease don't mind me.

I'm just the lady sitting next to you on the plane with tears streaming down my cheeks as we take off. The tension rising in my chest. The sob caught in my throat, so I don't cry out in the silence of our departure from the ground.

Because my son went to Heaven in January. And this is the closest I will physically get to him until my turn to go Home arrives.

Just before he passed, he had received the first aid and safety certification card required for flight school. Because he'd always wanted to fly. And he was going after that dream.

He was the kid we took to watch the planes take off at the nearby airport. The first one I ever took on a plane. And the one who could tell you all you needed to know about the planes at the air and space museums.

And here I sit. Crying on a plane. Trying not to grieve too loudly so as not to disturb everyone else's peace.

And watching the clouds pass by ... wishing I could reach out and touch him in heaven.

caleb in a cloud

In August of 2021, on my flight from Greenville/Spartanburg, South Carolina to Rochester, New York, I had a window seat. I have always loved watching the clouds go by on an airplane, as well as looking for shapes in them from the ground.

As we're flying, a cloud far off in the distance caught my eye, as it was alone on the horizon. I prepared to take some pictures of it.

Meanwhile, we're coming up on a cloud that had a wisp coming off the top of it, kind of like a curl of smoke or the perfect soft ice cream swirl. It was cool, and as much as I wanted to focus on the lonely cloud on the horizon, this wispy smoke cloud would not leave me alone. So, I snapped a bunch of shots of it as we flew past then took some of the horizon cloud.

When we landed in Philadelphia, Pennsylvania for a layover, I went looking for a toothbrush in the concessions shops. *Shopping trigger.* I had forgotten that *Rocky* was filmed in Philly, and the shop was full of *Rocky* paraphernalia. Since *Rocky* was one of Caleb's favorite movies, the grief caught in my throat and brought tears to my eyes once again. I picked out one of those metal pencil statues in the shape of Rocky posing victorious at the top of the stairs, hands raised with fists in the air. A souvenir to take back to

Caleb's gravesite. I grabbed a toothbrush, Combos, and a bottle of Cherry Coke and headed to find a seat to rest and wait for my next flight.

Once I finished taking pictures of the interesting sticker wall at the airport and got situated in my chair, I looked back at the shots I'd taken on the plane. That cloud had changed as I was shooting it ...

I found this:

I can hear God. "Hey Caleb, come here son. I have a special assignment for you today. Your mama needs to see you. Go sit behind that cloud over there and wave at your mama as she flies by."

When I've shown that photo to those who knew Caleb, I don't have to say anything. They see him right away. For those of you asking, "How do you know that's your son waving at you?"

Guess which one is Caleb.

This cloud photo was a God wink. Undeniably. Unmistakably. God winked at me (and so did Caleb, I would say) while I flew by on that plane, letting me know, once again, that He sees me, knows me, and cares for me in my grief and always.

surviving as a family

CHAPTER 32

marriage matters

Vic had been working in Savannah, Georgia for several months at the time of Caleb's passing. He would continue working four hours from home through September of 2021. Although grateful he was home when it happened, we had to face Vic's departure a couple weeks after the funeral.

For the next nine months, my husband travelled back and forth from Georgia to South Carolina on weekends. We grieved the death of our son hours apart from one another. He didn't get to come home from work each day to the comfort of a house full of people he loved, and we didn't have one another to hold in the evenings when all was quiet and our thoughts took off.

The hardest part of this for me was having to let him go every Sunday night. Many times, I'd wrap my arms around him and cry into his chest before releasing him to the highway, God's protection, and my prayers. Thankfully, he returned every weekend until the job was finished and he was able to move back home.

Rumor has it that marriages tend to take a hit after a child dies, whether the couple puts distance between themselves due to their separate ways of grieving, one blames the other for a child's accidental death, or they don't know how to adjust to this life without their child's presence.

I'd like to take a moment to dispel the lie that a majority of couples end up divorced after the loss of a child or repetitive child loss. The truth is that only twelve percent of marriages end in divorce after the loss of a child, and most of those divorces were documented for reasons other than child loss. On the flipside, twenty-five percent of marriages were reported as growing stronger after this life experience.[1]

Survival Tip:

Mama, prioritize your husband and both your grief journeys in this season. Doing so will protect your marriage and may even strengthen it. You will also find healing in the comfort you can bring each other. Here are several ways you can do this:

- **Write down what you want to say when you're both too busy and distant to talk.** This way, when you have time to connect, you don't have to struggle to recall it. Keep a mini composition notebook in your purse or someplace in your home where you have easy access to it when the phone rings.
- **When he's home, make time to be with him.** Don't schedule plans with other people or that will take you out of the home while he is present. Leave that time open for him and spend it together. Include the kids as much as you can, and if they have activities they must attend, have someone else take them.
- **Consider taking a peaceful getaway, even if it's only for a weekend.** You may even want to consider locating and attending a couples retreat for grieving parents.
- **If you had marital issues prior to the loss of your child, work through them together.** Seek trusted biblical counsel. Just as you aren't alone in your child loss, you aren't alone in needing to work on your

marriage. We all do. There's no shame in needing wise counsel. (Proverbs 11:14)

- **Take responsibility for your words and actions.** It's so easy to see the shortcomings in someone else, but we have a difficult time admitting to our own. We must focus on fixing ourselves, not our spouses. That's God's responsibility, not ours. (Luke 6:41-42)
- **Be quick to apologize for your mistakes.** Work toward pausing before you say anything when angry, frustrated, or annoyed. Count to ten before you speak. (Proverbs 17:27-28, Philippians 4:8-9)
- **Leave no room for the enemy to attack your relationship.** Don't go to bed angry. Kiss and make up before you go to sleep. (Ephesians 4:26-27)
- **Give one another grace.** None of us is perfect, and we all make mistakes. We all have our moments and our days. Make space for that in your lives. And repent if you see it becoming a habit, rather than an occasional hiccup. (Romans 5:20-21)

A Verse to Focus On:

Again, if two lie down together, they will keep warm;
But how can one be warm alone?
Though one may be overpowered by another, two can withstand him.
And a threefold cord is not quickly broken.
Ecclesiastes 4:11-12

Reflection:

What's one special thing you can plan for you and your husband to do during this difficult season?

CHAPTER 33

dad

Mama, your child's father needs the space to grieve as much as you and your kids do.

I don't know about yours, but my husband is a man's man. He's solid. Strong. Secure. Supportive. A rock in times of trouble. The one I turn to when I need a lifeline.

What we can't forget is that the dads of this world suffer as deeply from the death of their child as we mamas do. Although they are strong, this loss *will* bring them to their knees.

I wrote this note to Caleb one grief-filled afternoon:

Your dad's heart cries out too. Your departure has left a rather huge hole in his life. Not only did he lose a son, but he also lost a best friend. Someone who understood him and who he was because you were wired in so many of the same ways. Someone who listened to and practiced his advice, someone he discipled. Like Jesus wept when He lost John the Baptist, your father weeps.

Mama, pay attention to the father of your child. So many times, our men carry the weight of the world on their shoulders as they provide for us and their kids. This is one of those times we need to be certain that weight doesn't crush them. Be as aware of his grief as you are your own.

Maybe your husband is good at hiding his feelings. There are a few ways you can discern when he's under the weight of his grief:

- He's irritable more than usual.
- He's not enjoying things he normally does to relax or take a break.
- His temperament has changed.
- He says things he normally wouldn't say. Maybe these things hurt others.
- He's continuously going about life like nothing has happened (denial).

When you notice these things happening, acknowledge his needs for space, time, comfort, and empathy.

Survival Tip:

To be certain your husband has the opportunity to grieve as he needs, try the following:

- **Schedule one night each week to talk one-on-one for a heart check.**
- **Allow him time to do things he enjoys,** such as hunting or golfing or tinkering in the garage.
- **Encourage him to join his friends.** He needs the ability to process with another man. Especially if that man is another father who has lost a child.
- **Give him time to settle in after work.** Many husbands will come home from work, spend a few minutes in the car, and pray or decompress from the day. It allows him to leave work at work, rather than carrying the day's stressors into his home and relationships with his wife and kids. Suggest your

hubby do the same, but with the intention of
processing his grief. •

A Verse to Focus On:

Jesus wept.
John 11:35

Reflection:

What is one thing you've noticed your husband needs in order to
grieve well?

CHAPTER 34

stillness

One morning, a quiet stillness settled over our house, emphasizing the sadness I felt as I longed for the sounds of life and laughter to return.

Many facets of grief are difficult, but one of the hardest on a mama isn't necessarily managing her own grief; it's watching her children walk their grief journeys as the sibling of the deceased child. It's the sadness in their eyes. Watching them battle depression. The silent stares in place of the smiles and stories. The days when all they want to do is curl into a ball and stay in bed rather than do life. And having to encourage them to do life on those days, regardless of their grief.

Because school and work do not stop for grief. Life marches forward for all.

The cries of my children mourning their brother pierced my heart. I wanted to wrap them in my arms and hug the grief out of them while encouraging them to live fully as they took those steps away from the sorrow. But I am limited. My capacity is limited.

Since *I'm* not capable of healing them, I wrapped my arms around them, and we embraced like we'd never let go because letting go hurts too much. And I whispered a prayer to *Jehovah Rapha*, the One who *can* heal their hurt.

As that still morning passed, Hannah called to me from the living room. "Mama, come check this out."

I walked through the kitchen to find her standing next to a sunny outline of our window on the living room floor.

In the midst of it, a rainbow shimmered. God's symbol of hope for His children. His promise that this flood of tears won't take me out. Nor will the grief keep my children from finding His promises true in their lives.

Mama, I'm not going to lie. Next to the loss of your child, this is going to be one of the most heart-wrenching and difficult parts of your grief journey to handle.

Your children's grief will look similar to what you're experiencing but be entirely different in them. Their relationship with their sibling is different than your relationship with your son or daughter.

And just like you've been there for them when they've faced bullies or been ill or had their heart broken by a boy or a girl, you'll need to be there for them now. Just like you struggle to survive managing your household when you're sick with an illness, you'll struggle but survive managing while you're grieving.

Survival Tip:

Don't always hide your grief from your kids. Let them see that it's healthy to cry, laugh, rest, groan, use a punching bag, take a walk, talk about the loved one who is gone, and everything else that is a healthy grieving activity. Pull them close and grieve together. *Heal together*.

What's one thing about your grief that you can safely share with your children without adding to their trauma? Make the time to share with them and open a discussion about their grieving process.

A Verse to Focus On:

Blessed are those who mourn,
For they shall be comforted.
Matthew 5:4

Reflection:

What are you hiding from your children in an attempt to ease their grieving process?

sibling similarities

One afternoon, I snuck into Gideon's room to check on him, as I hadn't seen him yet that day. I found him peacefully sleeping, but I did a double take. At first glance, he looked just like Caleb.

There have been more occasions where Gideon has reminded me of his brother. Some of his actions and mannerisms are similar. When scrolling my phone, there are photos of them that catch my breath as Gideon grows taller and opts for similar haircuts to what his brother had. They look *so much* alike.

I'm not the only one who has noticed the similarities, either. Friends and family have pointed it out. Concerned this may disturb Gideon, I asked him, "Does it bother you that others look at you and see Caleb at times?" He responded it didn't, and I breathed a sigh of relief. One less thing for me to worry about.

It's a normal part of the grieving process to notice the similarities between the child you lost and those who remain. It's also normal to recognize the differences and miss what is lacking in the family dynamic.

However, it's important to note that our remaining children cannot replace their deceased sibling in our lives—nor should they be asked or required to do so. When those thoughts cross our minds, we must quickly shove them aside. Each of our children are unique and need to be loved for who they are, not overlooked for, or asked to replace, who they aren't. It's not fair to our children to depend on them to fill the hole their sibling left.

Survival Tip:

When you find yourself seeking comfort in the similarities between your surviving children and the one you miss, try the following to take the focus off that desire for replacement:

- **Define what is missing.** Is it the way your child hugged you? How he or she sought your advice then took it? The way their smile lit up their eyes? Their consideration for others? Defining what's missing will help you to recognize how special that trait was in the child you are grieving.
- **Step away from the situation.** Before seeking out a similarity in your child's sibling, pause. Take a deep breath. Don't say anything to your surviving child. Not yet. Consider how your actions or words may affect your child.
- **Think of something you love about the child you're trying to compare with the one you miss.** Focus on that quality or trait and consider how much joy he or she brings you.
- **Go back to the situation at hand.** Allow him or her your full attention. Be sure to express your love for them and encourage the trait you admire in them.

A Verse to Focus On:

For I consider that the sufferings of this present time are not worthy to be compared with the glory which shall be revealed in us.
Romans 8:18

Reflection:

What unique traits do you admire in each of your children?

CHAPTER 36

the aftermath – fight

Hannah's response to grief was to fight. Mostly with her words. Her aggression was the hardest expression of grief I experienced.

I would take her to work at the clothing store where it was her responsibility to keep the fitting rooms cleaned and the clothing organized throughout the store. Occasionally, she would help a customer or run the register. Grief caused her extreme anxiety when it came time to drop her off for work. She would refuse to get out of the truck, have panic attacks, and ugly cry.

At home, it wasn't much better. If she wasn't holed up in her room, she would spout negativity, argue we were yelling at her when we provided simple instruction or asked her to do a chore, and run off at the mouth about how she wished she could move out.

Probably the hardest thing to watch her go through was walking away from the Lord for a season. We couldn't tell if she was mad at God, questioning her faith in Him, or just wanted a break from the social aspects of church. At one point, she confessed that every time she entered the sanctuary, it triggered her grief. We'd had Caleb's Celebration of Life at the church, and we had an open-casket viewing prior to the event. She saw the casket every time she entered the sanctuary. This, I could understand.

Another tragedy at her age is that she is an adult, so she has the right to accept or deny any treatment. Hannah didn't want to go to counseling. As she put it, "I don't want to talk to a stranger." She didn't want to talk with those of us she knew, either. Except Grandma.

Children will experience grief when a sibling dies, no matter their age. Whether they are three or twenty, they may not be able to express their feelings. Hannah had a difficult time processing her grief, and it surfaced as temper tantrums, anger, frustration, and depression. We didn't know what to expect from her one day to the next.

Survival Tip:

When your child is in fight mode, it's easy to become worn out. Mama, self-care is necessary for you in this season. I know I've said this before, but it's truly that important. It's like the airline oxygen mask dropping down in case of an emergency. You must put on your mask so you can keep breathing to help others do the same. If you don't, you'll stop breathing before you can help.

Here are some ways to help your child when he or she is in fight mode:

- **Don't judge.** It's easy to judge someone else's frustration or anger. When all someone sees is red, and we see the light, we want to make them see it too. But until they can shut down the red, they won't be able to see what we do.
- **Give your child space to process.** Some won't be willing to share, and we have to be okay with that. Given space and time, he or she may open up. If not, be aware of that, as well, and seek counsel. Maybe a

trusted adult outside of the family—or Grandma—will be a safe sounding board for your child's grief. By giving them space, I'm not saying to allow them to isolate. We want our children to be safe, not suicidal. Be acutely aware of your child's process and what they do behind closed doors in this season. Take the door off its hinges, if necessary. But allow him or her space.

- **Be gentle, and don't react.** We cannot allow one child to set the tone in our homes. Ask God to give you strength and peace so you can maintain a restful environment. Respond to your child's anger with kindness and gentleness. Usually, a gentle word will diffuse the situation. If not, ask your son or daughter to please go to their room until they can speak respectfully to others in the household.

A Verse to Focus On:

Why then have You brought me out of the womb?
Oh, that I had perished and no eye had seen me!
Job 10:18

Reflection:

What is something kind you could say to your child to reassure him or her of your love, God's love, and that he or she will be okay?

the aftermath – flight

Mama, facing new medical issues makes this grief journey that much more difficult to navigate. There's nothing like having grief piled onto grief. And that's exactly what new medical issues stir up in us: grief. We want nothing more than for our children be healed and healthy. We spend hours praying for their bodies and minds to realign with their divine design.

Driving to that initial doctor's appointment, receiving diagnoses, looking down the treatments and trials road, having to try different meds, and all the future appointments are enough to weary a mama's soul all on their own. Let alone coupled with the death of a child looming beneath it all.

Prior to Caleb's death, Ezra had struggled with depression and social anxiety. He'd been bullied in middle school, and his relationship with his dad was a struggle for them both for many years. We believe the bullying stunted his mental, emotional, and social development in some ways.

The most peculiar aspect of Ezra's struggle was the way he'd clasp his hands together in front of him, tuck his chin, raise his shoulders, and grin real big every time he was excited. We'd told him more than once he shouldn't do that in front of his peers, because they would pick on him for it. He'd told us he couldn't help it. After hearing this a handful of times and observing the tic, I realized he was telling me the truth. His body did it despite his best efforts to resist.

Up until Caleb's death, this was the only tic Ezra had, and it was entirely physical.

Trauma can be a major trigger for people with Tourette's Syndrome. Ezra went from one physical tic to many and the addition of vocal tics. As a result, he's had difficulty getting and keeping work. This led to frustration, deferred hope, depression, and insomnia. Tourette's is also painful, as his muscles are constantly tensing and releasing with the physical attacks. Sometimes, he tries holding back the verbal tics, which causes another level of pain.

As a mama, it's been hard watching my son struggle. His deepest desire is to live a normal life: get up and go to work, play video games to relax, and get a good night of sleep on a consistent basis. But the Tourette's prevents that from becoming a reality right now. We're hopeful that one day—sooner than later—he'll find some semblance of normal. But like Covid did for many, he, Vic, and I are having to learn to live with a new normal.

Survival Tip:

Mama, your child's sanity is your first priority in this situation. If you notice he or she is in flight mode, running from grief and any other issues he or she is facing, or struggling with a new additional circumstance in his or her life, it's important they know you're there for them in this season. To do this, you can:

- **Be available to talk when they're ready to do so.**
  Make sure you stop whatever you're doing and focus
  on what your child is sharing. Make eye contact. This
  allows your child to know you are present in the
  moment with him or her. It also demonstrates how
  much you care for them.
- **Speak his or her love language.** Whether it's
  physical touch, words of affirmation, quality time,
  acts of service, or gifts, making it a point to refill your
  child's love tank may help ground them, provide
  stability, bring an ounce of healing, and draw them
  out of flight mode.
- **Be present for appointments.** This helps a child feel
  safe and secure. This also helps to take the pressure off
  when they're asked a question and may not know
  how to answer it.

Here's a way to manage the medical side of grief:

- **Get a notebook.** Label it with your family member's
  name and what issue you're managing. Take notes at
  every appointment. Document every phone call, every
  doctor's name, every medication and the dosage
  details, every exam, every session, and every test. Write
  down appointment dates and times. This way, you
  have all of the information you could possibly need
  for every question medical professionals or social
  services personnel could ask.
- **Get a folder and label that too.** Keep all
  documents, receipts, and other related items in this
  folder so that they are at your fingertips. You can keep
  a digital file, of course, but if you are handed physical
  paper documents and receipts, I highly recommend a
  physical file you can take to appointments with you.

- **Keep the notebook and journal together where you can easily reference them and grab and go.**
- **Set appointment reminders and alarms on your phone so you don't forget.** This will help with the grief fog.

A Verse to Focus On:

My heart is in turmoil and cannot rest;
Days of affliction confront me.
Job 30:27

Reflection:

What is one way you've seen grief physically manifest in your loved ones' lives? What feelings does that stir up?

CHAPTER 38

the aftermath – freeze

S ome people suffer loss in silence. But grief has a way of rising to the surface, even in the strong, silent types.

The day before the eight-month anniversary of Caleb's death started according to my plans, but it didn't end that way.

Gideon was taking German that year. And that day happened to be the day they learned how to say brother. *Bruder.* He had to write his sibling's names *and locations.* Imagine him having to write *Caleb. Heaven.* It broke him.

By the end of third block, he was in a full-blown panic attack. He suffered through fourth block and finally, at 3:15PM, he told me he was having this attack. Chest pain that comes in unbearable waves. Difficult breaths. *In. Out. In. Out.* Nausea triggered by the pain as every muscle tenses.

Gideon suffered these panic attacks for several months. The resolution? Relationship. They stopped when he met his high school sweetheart.

Survival Tip:

Mama, we don't know how grief will affect our kids until it

does. And then, the best way to manage it is to do what we can and leave the rest in God's hands.

- **Connect.** Even if your child can't find a way to express him or herself, knowing that you are focused on them matters. Take time to make eye contact. Do an activity together that your child will enjoy; help take their mind off their grief and provide opportunity for him or her to feel an opposite emotion. Tell your child you love him or her.
- **Take a break.** Each of you is living under the stressors of everyday life with grief piled on top. Get outside where there's fresh air and sunshine. Breathe deep. Look for the beauty around you. Help your child find a treasure to put in his pocket or her hair. Take a moment to enjoy life together.
- **Rest.** Make time in your and your children's schedules for rest. Our bodies aren't designed to run nonstop. That's why God created the Sabbath, a day to stop all work and rest. You may need to pull your child from an activity for a season, take a family vacation, or just spend an afternoon away from school and work. The important thing here is to make time for rest.

Remember, Mama, it's okay to take a break from grief. Our kids need that as much as we do, if not more.

A Verse to Focus On:

Return to your rest, O my soul,
For the LORD has dealt bountifully with you.
Psalm 116:7

Reflection:

What's one way you can connect with your child in the middle of his or her grieving process?

CHAPTER 39

restless

Mama, it's likely there will come a point during this grief process that you or someone in your household will want to make a life-altering decision.

Vic wanted to quit his stressful job as a concrete construction superintendent on a daily basis. He was concerned the duress would cause a heart attack, and I'd be left alone.

There were several times that year when I wanted to sell everything we own, move into an RV, and travel across the country. After all, we don't know how long—or short—our lives may be, and I wanted to make more memories with my husband. But it wasn't time for that, either. Not yet.

We still have young adults at home, and we aren't financially prepared for either of those life-changing choices.

Mama, every choice we make has a consequence. Making life-changing choices based on a strong emotion is *never* a wise idea. Surviving the year of firsts after our loss is hard enough without heaping additional stressors on top of the grief.

Granted, there will be circumstances that will require an immediate decision, such as needing to move closer to family because you need someone to lean on in this difficult season or something happened in your home that makes it impossible to live there. But most life-altering decisions can wait until you aren't as immersed in grief as you are today.

Survival Tip:

If you find that you or your family members are restless, it's time to call a family gathering. Try the following agenda:

- **Pray together before you begin your conversation.** Acknowledge the restlessness in your home and ask God to provide His peace that passes all understanding.
- **Announce that you've noticed the restlessness.** Note that after a life-changing event, it's normal to feel this way.
- **Give everyone time to discuss how they are feeling and any concerns they may have.** Take turns talking. Be sure to acknowledge each family member's response. Everyone needs to be heard.
- **Address the concerns.** Is what each one has expressed something that is in his or her control? If not, discuss the importance of not dwelling on it and allowing room for God to do what He needs to do in our hearts and minds.
- **Brainstorm alternative, non-life-altering options that will satisfy the restlessness.** Remind everyone, including yourself, that it isn't wise to make these types of decisions for the first year of your grieving process.
- **Pray again.** Ask God to move in these areas and to provide wisdom over the next year.
- **You could also resort to the age-old list of pros and cons.** Writing down the potential consequences of leaving a job or moving elsewhere helps us see reality through our emotional unrest.

A Verse to Focus On:

Likewise the Spirit also helps in our weaknesses. For we do not know what we should pray for as we ought, but the Spirit Himself makes intercession for us with groanings which cannot be uttered. Now He who searches the hearts knows what the mind of the Spirit is, because He makes intercession for the saints according to the will of God. Romans 8:26-27

Reflection:

What is one temptation you've faced since your child's death? List ten realistic, safe ways you can resolve that temptation.

surviving the firsts

CHAPTER 40

mother's day

Mama, most of this book came from the social media posts I'd written that first year after Caleb's death. While going back through them, I discovered I never posted about Mother's Day. It's like I skipped right over it, ignored it, or just didn't participate.

Or maybe I did, but instead of mourning my motherhood and the loss I'd suffered, I chose to focus on the present and the children who still call me Mom on a daily basis.

I confess, that first Mother's Day without Caleb, I didn't really feel like participating. Although still a mom to five young adults, my heart wasn't into celebrating motherhood. And I honestly can't remember what I did or didn't do. Did Vic take me out for dinner? Possibly. I know the kids didn't take me out for dinner. I would have documented that occasion. Did I focus on celebrating my own mom? Likely.

My point is, we're the mamas. It's our day to reflect on being the person who birthed our children, nurtured them, supported and encouraged them, and raised them to make their impact on this world, no matter how long or how short that time would be. It's also okay if we don't feel like celebrating this day for a season or two.

Survival Tip:

Mama, your heart is broken. There's a large hole in it where your child once fully lived. And nothing and no one else can fill that void. Mother's Day festivities—or lack thereof—are entirely your choice. Set a boundary based on how you feel, not how everyone else feels. You could:

- **Take the day off.** If you don't want to celebrate Mother's Day, then don't. Hide in your secret place and allow the Lord to minister comfort to that broken place in you.
- **Put the focus on your mother or your spouse's mother.** Maybe you've lost your mother, too, but you know a woman who you'd consider to be your second mama. Take the focus off yourself and serve someone else. When I do this, I find joy in those broken places.
- **Celebrate life in its fullness.** That grief is going to be present for a long time. We never truly get over a loss like this. But life will continue. Our surviving kids need us, our love, and our attentions and affections as much as their sibling did. Focus on them. Let them love on you for a day. And allow their laughter, jokes, gifts, words of affirmation, hugs, kisses, and lives to minister to that broken place in you and bring the light of life back into your eyes.

Every Mother's Day, I try to get a picture with my kids. Sometimes it's as a group, sometimes individually, sometimes both. Flipping back through them, I cherish the moments each particular year. The times we went out to eat. The times we gathered with my mom and sister and her family. The year we adopted Victoria was a particular favorite. And even the year Caleb was missing for the first time.

Life is full of joy and heartache. It's what you choose to do with it that will lead to abundance or lack. I pray you choose abundance this Mother's Day, Mama.

A Verse to Focus On:

Surely He has borne our griefs
And carried our sorrows ...
Isaiah 53:4

Reflection:

How are you truly feeling this Mother's Day? Write down a favorite Mother's Day memory from before your child passed.

CHAPTER 41

special occasions

Within the first year after Caleb's death, his sister and cousin graduated from high school, and one of his friends got married. Within the second year after, another of his friends became a father. While Caleb had graduated from high school and gotten engaged, we missed out on his wedding and, potentially, our grandchildren.

Mama, special occasions can trigger some deep hurt if your child isn't present to participate in these milestone events in life.

When Josh and Shayla brought their son Noadiah to church for the first time, they'd given me a heads up that they were coming, and I waited close to the doors in anticipation of their arrival. The joy of meeting one of my son's best friend's babies filled my heart. I patiently watched as Shayla freed him from his stroller. When she handed Noadiah to me, I spent minutes admiring his sweet face, and then it hit me. Hard. The overwhelming joy of new life crashed with the grief of knowing I would never experience being a grandma to Caleb's children. This first meeting would never happen.

The sobbing choked its way into my throat as tears filled my eyes to overflowing, and I cried and snotted, trying not to drip on baby Noadiah. Josh rubbed my back and gave me a side hug, understanding in his eyes. "Are you okay, Mama?" Yep. I would be just fine, I nodded. "I get it," he told me.

The grief of child loss is such a dichotomy. There are going to be many moments going forward where joy and grief will collide in life. Allowing joy to win the battle is the key to surviving, Mama.

Survival Tip:

When special occasions arrive, try to find ways to include your son or daughter in these events. For example:

Graduations:

- **Decorate a chair.** Ask your child's high school or college administration for permission. Lay out your son's or daughter's cap and gown, tassel, any cords they've earned, their diploma cover, a framed photo, and anything that represents their accomplishments or extracurricular activities. Be sure to respect any boundaries provided by the administration.
- **Ask if someone may walk in your child's place and receive his or her diploma in your child's stead.**
- **Create a scholarship fund in your child's name and memory.** Select a particular extracurricular activity your child participated in and give the money to a graduating senior who also participated in this activity. Select a senior who had a GPA similar to your child's. Was he or she headed to college or university? See if any other seniors are going to the same one and split the funds amongst them or choose one to give it to. Have the senior class write essays on what matters most in life and how they plan to honor that in their

futures. Choose one to bless with the scholarship
fund. There are so many things you could do here.

- **Take photos of siblings and Photoshop your son
  or daughter into the picture.** When my daughter
  graduated, her brother's absence was difficult for her.
  When we took her senior portraits, we went to the
  same place I had taken his. This enabled me to easily
  place Caleb into a few of them, leaving her feeling as if
  he was present, in a way.

Weddings:

- **Accept invitations to participate.** When Caleb's
  friend Jed married, he asked Victor to be a
  groomsman. We knew Vic was standing in for Caleb.
  But the invitation to do so left us blessed and feeling
  as if Caleb was honored at this special event.
- **Create an honorary seat at the wedding and
  reception.** When our friends' daughter got married, a
  seat in the midst of the family held a framed photo of
  her deceased brother and was decorated to hold his
  space.
- **Purchase an extra gift and give it in the name of
  your son or daughter.** What would your child have
  given his sibling or her best friend? Purchase that and
  a card and sign it from him or her.

Baby Showers:

- **Consider bringing a gift that represents your son
  or daughter.** Most moms are asking for books
  instead of cards these days. Purchase a copy of the
  book your son or daughter enjoyed when you read to
  them and include your child's name in the signature.

A Verse to Focus On:

And let us consider one another in order to stir up love and good works, not forsaking the assembling of ourselves together, as is the manner of some, but exhorting one another, and so much the more as you see the Day approaching.
Hebrews 10:24-25

Reflection:

What are three ways you can serve others during their special events, even if it means not being able to incorporate the memory of your son or daughter? Is there something you can do for them in honor of your child?

CHAPTER 42

grieving together

As I sat at my worktable in my home office one early morning in June of 2021, I noticed I'd missed a call from Beth, one of my best friends who'd sat with Vic and me the entire week of Caleb's funeral. She and her husband, Danny, were present every spare moment they had while we mourned the loss of our son.

She'd left a message, and as I listened, my heart sank, and the reality of child loss returned as if I'd just received that call all over again. Danny's son, Mason, had died that morning. I immediately returned her call and listened as she poured out her grief. Beth loved Mason as her own, despite the label of being his stepmom. My plans for that week were cancelled, and Vic and I focused on being there for our friends as they'd been there for us.

It amazes me how God will take us through something so we can then walk through it alongside someone else. How He uses the comfort we received in a time of need to provide comfort for a friend in their time of need. How He takes our pain and give us purpose in it.

As Vic and I sat with Beth and Danny that week, as we prayed and held space for them, God ministered more healing and comfort to my own heart. The pain of my grief had the ability to ease the pain of another's in the sense of being able to be there for her as she endured her own. She knew someone close to her had experienced the same grief, and it brought comfort to her.

Mama, every time a friend or family member loses a child, it will stir your grief. Take heart. You are not alone. It's like buying a new car. When you buy that car, you start to see all the other cars of the same make and model on the road. When you become a mother who has suffered child loss, you become acutely aware of other moms you know who have also experienced it.

Survival Tip:

If the day comes that you need to sit with a friend in their grief, be prepared to say yes. Then, apply the following tips:

- **Share your testimony.** Allow God to use it to heal and comfort others. Beth shared multiple times with her friends and family that we'd lost a child six months before. Just our presence in their grief testified to them and others that survival was possible.
- **Remind them to ask for help.** Remember that first week and how much needed to be done and how foggy your brain was with grief. Sometimes we like to do it all ourselves because we know what we want. Sometimes we don't, but we forget that we can ask for help. Give your loved ones a gentle nudge and let them know you're there to serve them.
- **Serve your loved ones.** Offer to clean the kitchen so they can rest. Make the run to the grocery store. Water all the plants that have been delivered to their home. Warm up the casseroles. Entertain the children while they focus on making arrangements.
- **Take a step back.** Part of being a servant is knowing when someone doesn't need your help. Don't try too hard to share your experiences or tell them how to

make their own arrangements. Give them space and wait for them to ask for help again.

- **Pray.** Not just for them, but for yourself too. Stepping into someone else's grief after you've suffered your own is no easy task. Give the burden to Jesus, ask God to protect your heart, mind, and spirit, and be prepared for your own grief to trigger. This is most important.
- **Obey God's prompting.** If you hear the Lord whisper a directive, a Scripture, or anything else to your heart, heed His voice. Victor ended up sharing a scripture verse with Danny, and it ministered to Danny in that moment. God can and will use you to bring healing. Obedience to His prompting is key.

A Verse to Focus On:

Blessed be the God and Father of our Lord Jesus Christ, the Father of mercies and God of all comfort, who comforts us in all our tribulation, that we may be able to comfort those who are in any trouble, with the comfort with which we ourselves are comforted by God.
2 Corinthians 1:3-4

Reflection:

What's one way God has brought healing to your heart through either someone else's testimony or the sharing of your own?

caleb's birthday

C aleb was born on November 19, 2001. Opening day of deer season in New York. Thanksgiving week. We had plans to travel to my grandparents that week, as we traditionally did. It was a four-hour car ride. Vic had looked forward to hunting on Grandpa's hill that day and reminded me multiple times that month that I needed to wait to give birth to our son until after the holiday. God and Caleb had other plans, and we found ourselves welcoming our little buck into our lives that opening day.

I knew in my mother's heart from the moment he entered the world that Caleb was going to be independent and strong willed. He didn't bond with me the way my other three bonded. And that was okay. God made me fully aware of Caleb's character and personality in those early moments with my son, which would prove helpful as he grew and I parented.

My biggest fear has always been that one of our children wouldn't outlive Vic and me. Caleb tested my trust in the Lord from the day we left the hospital. Vic had already gone ahead to my grandparents. My mom was going to pick up me and Caleb from the hospital when she finished her school day, and we would make the drive out together. It was hours before we were to be discharged when the medical team informed me that Caleb had a heart murmur, and they'd scheduled us with a pediatric cardiologist. Thankfully, the cardiologist's office was the same distance from my grandparents' as it was from home. We found out that week that the small hole in his heart was the type that typically healed within a few years (and did).

That fear didn't end with the healing of his heart, though. No. Caleb had multiple wild streaks that would challenge my own heart for years to come. I could tell you some stories. For nineteen years, one month, and fifteen days, I wondered if and when …

the first birthday

A few months before Caleb's birthday barged into my calendar, I began considering what we could do to honor his life. Going on an adventure would make sense, but I wasn't in the mood for such a thing. Instead, Vic and I decided we would gather friends and family and celebrate one more time. I confess. I selfishly wanted life and laughter in our home. I didn't want to spend all day mourning and wishing and going *there*. Caleb wouldn't want me to do that either.

We invited family and close friends of ours and Caleb's to our home. Grandma and Grandpa Johnson arrived first, the fresh scent of homemade cherry pie wafting from her insulated casserole carrier. Once our family members were present, we picked up our forks and ate from the center of the pie together, just as Caleb would. An hour later, his friends arrived. That evening, we did a few things: shared stories, wrote down favorite memories, and took pictures. It was a wonderful evening filled with laughter, a few tears, and plenty of hugs. Had he been there in person, Caleb would have loved it.

Survival Tip:

Mama, as your child's earthly birthday arrives, consider what you could do to celebrate his or her life. Here are a few suggestions to get the ideas flowing:

- **Host a gathering of family and friends and share stories.**
- **Have a picnic at your child's gravesite or favorite outdoor location.**
- **Go on an adventure.** Even if it's a local hike or a trip to the beach.
- **Paint rocks.** Design them with your child's favorite things or sayings and leave them in his or her favorite places for others to find some joy in their day.
- **Do something that serves someone or something else.** Plant a tree or make a donation to a charity or adopt a puppy in your child's name.
- **Host a scrapbooking/memory-keeping party.** Print off a bunch of pictures of your child throughout their lifetime and invite family and friends over to create memory books or albums with them.
- **Order your child's favorite takeout.** Make it a movie night and curl up on the couch to watch his or her favorite.

Whatever you choose, find something to do that brings you joy and takes the focus off the fact that your child is no longer present to celebrate.

A Verse to Focus On:

The end of a thing is better than its beginning ...
Do not say,
"Why were the former days better than these?"
For you do not inquire wisely concerning this.
Ecclesiastes 7:8a, 10

Reflection:

What fond memories do you have of your child's birthday throughout the years? Write them down.

CHAPTER 44

Thanksgiving

Thanksgiving 2021 was wonderful. It wasn't as sad as I expected it to be eating without one of our children at the table. Maybe it's because I saw a social media post that reminded me whose table Caleb would be present at, and that made me smile more than I wanted to cry. That post set me up for a day full of life and tasty food. And dance parties with the Wii. I could still hold my own against my children, consistently coming in third. I still had the moves! I'm just glad they invited me to play and didn't mind sweating with this oldie.

I was blessed and thankful for so many things that season, despite our loss.

- My husband and the trooper he'd been that year, as he worked away from home for nine months while grieving our loss. It was *not* an easy season for him on all fronts. In God's strength, he made it through. He remains my hero.

- Our kids. They're growing and maturing into adults who will make their impacts on this world. Because of them, my grief doesn't swallow me. They are a light in my world.

- Our church family. Hope Church Spartanburg remains one of my favorite faith homes on this planet, second only to Catskill Mountain Christian Center. It's rare to find such a caring ministry team who truly love the Lord and His Word, which translates into loving people well. I'm blessed to know them.

- My friends. They held me up that year and many years before and after. I remain truly blessed by my sisters in the Lord and in life.

- We had a roof over our heads and gas in our cars and food on our tables. Because God provides for His children. Praise the Lord!

- Memories. Life isn't about what we have in the physical realm. It's about what we have in the spiritual and relational realms. I'm grateful that I'm in relationship with so many wonderful people and that I was able to stay home with and raise my children. It's the memories that carry us through the losses in life. We must make good ones!

- My job. I love the authors I've worked with in my writing and editing career. A few have become friends and encourage me as well. Is it work when you enjoy it?

Mama, there is so much to be thankful for in life. We just have to look for it. Sometimes when you're in the midst of a storm, it's hard to see your hand in front of your face. But even when you can't see it, you know it's there. You can feel its presence. It's a part of you.

It's the same with the Lord, His light, joy, and thankfulness. They're all present. Even when we cannot see them. But we can feel them in our hearts. We can sense their presence. We know without a doubt they're part of us. And we can choose to acknowledge them even when we doubt or lose sight or find bitterness creeping up in our souls. I pray you find these things today, despite the current storms in your life.

Survival Tip:

Gratitude shouldn't be something we only focus on in the month of November as Thanksgiving rolls around. Rather, it's something God desires of us daily. Moment by moment.

When you find yourself slipping into sadness, depression, or deep grief, put on a garment of praise. Thank the Lord for His goodness in your life. I know it's difficult to be grateful in grief, so here are a few prompts for you to find those things to be grateful for:

- **Do you have breath in your lungs today?** Were you able to get out of bed? Can you hug someone? Think about your physical body. What are you grateful for? (Now is *not* the time to focus on your weight gain or illness or negative self-image.)
- **Is there a roof over your head?** Food on your table? A car that gets you from point A to point B? Do you have hot, running water? Electricity? A bed to sleep in? Sometimes we tend to overlook all that God provides for us as something to be grateful for.
- **Who is in your life that you appreciate?** Yes, you've lost a child, maybe a parent, a friend. But that should never detract from the relationships that remain. Who are you grateful for today?
- **Step outside and look around you.** What is beautiful? Where do you see God in His creation?

We don't always have to dig deep to be grateful. When you struggle to find something to be grateful for, keep it simple. I find that when I start to praise God for who He is and the simple things He has blessed me with, gratitude for the deeper things begins to pour forth. Start simple, Mama.

A Verse to Focus On:

For the LORD will comfort Zion,
He will comfort all her waste places;
He will make her wilderness like Eden,
And her desert like the garden of the LORD;
Joy and gladness will be found in it,
Thanksgiving and the voice of melody.
Isaiah 51:3

Reflection:

Take a moment to reflect on what God has done in your life over the past year. What do you have to be grateful for? What attributes of His character are you thankful He has allowed you to witness this year?

CHAPTER 45

holiday hibernation

I thought it was a great idea to take a retail job at a craft store as a way to keep my mind off my grief as our first holiday season without Caleb swung into full gear. I figured I would serve customers with a smile and an encouraging word as I admired their Christmas décor choices and wondered what creations would come of their craft supplies, just as I'd done in seasons past.

But just a few days into the job, I discovered I wasn't much of a people person. Several times a day, I would ask customers, "How are you?" Then they would ask how I was. And because I didn't want to dampen someone else's holiday spirit, I would say, "I'm okay." Truth is, I wasn't really okay.

While people were out buying their kids presents, I was mourning that I wouldn't be purchasing any for Caleb. While wrapping gifts for my surviving kids and hubby, I had to take multiple breaks because of a full awareness I wasn't writing Caleb's name on any gift tags.

I was exhausted. I wanted to curl up into a fetal position in the warmth and comfort of my bed and not come out until the flowers did. I missed my boy too much. My heart couldn't take it. I spent the entire season wishing I hadn't taken that position.

Everything wore me out. My tone was bitter at times, and I

lacked the patience I typically walk in. I knew it was grief. But I disliked my reactions because bitterness has never been my style. Joy was harder to find despite it being my favorite time of the year. I physically felt the weight of grief bearing down on me, bringing utter exhaustion with it. I didn't want to be around bubbly people. I wanted to spend time alone with my tears. I dragged myself to church instead of wanting to be there. Life was backward and upside down.

What I came to realize was that I was no longer simply grieving. I was now under the oppression of a spirit of grief.

Survival Tip:

Mama, I didn't finish this part of my story here, because it wasn't over yet. God didn't work that grief spirit out until a little later in my journey. I will share that with you shortly, but for now, let's focus on how to make it through a season where grief is bearing down, and you just want to hibernate for the remainder of it.

- **Be aware of what you are experiencing on all levels.** Emotionally, physically, mentally, and spiritually. Note if any of these symptoms are worsening. If so, talk to a healthcare professional— either your primary care doctor or a therapist.
- **Don't take on extra during the seasons that are important to you and/or were important to your child.** Especially the first year. You will likely be on a roller coaster ride with grief and don't need to burden yourself with more than you can handle. It's okay to say "no."
- **Mentally prepare yourself for the activities you choose to participate in.** Remind yourself that it's okay to live, to enjoy, and to celebrate. Have a plan to excuse yourself if you become overwhelmed at any

time. Maybe you just need a few minutes to cry it out, fix your makeup, and return to the festivities. Maybe you will need to call it a night. Either way, know that you are okay, your decision is okay, and those who truly care will understand.

• **Take a day for yourself when needed.** You don't have to be strong. You don't have to push through this season. You do need to take care of yourself. Hibernate for a day.

A Verse to Focus On:

Keep your heart with all diligence,
For out of it spring the issues of life.
Proverbs 4:23

Reflection:

What can you leave off your plate this Christmas? What freedom do you need so you have room to grieve?

CHAPTER 46

christmas Traditions

I t's been our family tradition since I was a child to allow the kids to retrieve their stockings at any hour of the night on Christmas Eve, but they aren't allowed to touch the presents under the tree until we're all gathered Christmas morning.

Being our first year without Caleb, I didn't want to leave his stocking packed in the bin I store them in throughout the year. I wanted to hang it with everyone else's. I also didn't want to leave it hanging empty while the rest of ours hung stuffed full.

I thought and prayed about what to do with it, and I decided to fill it with gifts for everyone else that I thought Caleb might have given them if he were still with us.

I bought his dad and brothers Dr. Squatch Star Wars series soap. Hannah got a set of sushi magnets, and Tori received a ball cap with a fishhook attached to the rim.

Putting presents under the tree was fairly easy. Stuffing everyone else's stockings was a cinch. But when I got to Caleb's ...

As I pulled it from its hook, the dam broke. The biggest, wettest tears I'd cried all year streamed down my cheeks and splattered as they hit the floor. I hugged his stocking to my chest and let the grief flow. My shoulders shuddered as I sniffled big and tried not to cry out and wake the rest of my household, who had turned in for the night.

Except Zachary. Zach was sleeping on our couch during his visit, and he stood and wrapped his arms around me and just held me while I cried. Such a tender moment for me as a stepmom. Another simple touch from God bringing comfort to my sorrow.

After several minutes, the tears subsided, and I was able to stuff the stocking and hang it back in its rightful spot on the mantle. I added the new Spongebob ornament I'd purchased to the hook with the stocking and stepped back to admire the evidence of God's gift of life hanging before me. Eight full stockings. I counted the blessing of my marriage, which has survived twenty-three years of ups and downs, trials and successes, heated disagreements and joy. And the six beautiful children we've raised and poured into along the journey.

Survival Tip:

Mama, Christmas is full of family traditions. Take an account of yours. What traditions have been passed down from generation to generation? What ones have you and your husband created for your own family? What traditions have your kids created on their own?

Some traditions, such as filling the stockings was for me, may be a trigger of your grief this year. Is there a creative way you can alter the tradition to make it more bearable? Or do you want to keep it as it's been and allow the grief to flow?

What traditions could you alter now that a child is gone? What new traditions could you add in memory of your child?

These are a few questions to consider as you prepare for your first Christmas without your son or daughter. Whatever you decide, have peace in knowing that you are choosing what is best for your family for this year.

A Verse to Focus On:

I am weary with my crying;
My throat is dry;
My eyes fail while I wait for my God.
Psalm 69:3

Reflection:

What's your favorite holiday tradition? Where did it start? What's your fondest memory of participating in this tradition? Can you remember a time when your child enjoyed celebrating it as well?

CHAPTER 47

The one year anniversary

On Sunday, January 2, 2022, I wept through worship at Hope Church. That morning, the anniversary date of Caleb's accident, hope seemed a far-off wish. Most of my thoughts were on Caleb and my grief. For weeks, I'd felt depressed, unable to pull myself out of the funk overwhelming me. No matter how hard I tried, I just couldn't find the joy I desired.

As worship ended, Pastor Rich took the stage and called out a spirit of grief, then prayed over the congregation against that spirit. I felt an *immediate* shift inside of me.

Mama, sometimes we grieve. And sometimes a spirit of grief attaches itself to us.

How do I know the difference?

Grieving comes and goes. You'll be okay one day and not okay the next. Maybe it will linger a day or two or three, but it won't move in. A spirit of grief will overwhelm you for an extended period of time. You'll struggle to turn off a spirit of grief. When you're simply grieving, you'll be able to turn it off like flipping a switch. A spirit of grief will take your thoughts captive to your loss and will grip your heart without relenting. You are able to control your thoughts and refocus on life instead of death when you are simply grieving.

If this is what you're experiencing, it's time for deliverance from the spirit of grief. Find yourself a pastor, family member, or friend who knows how to go to battle for you and can pray effectively for that spirit to release its grip on you. Keep in mind that at the name of Jesus, every knee will bow.

Sometimes we humans like to hang out in our storms. Although we feel like we're sinking, we fear what may come if we don't hang on tight to the things we know and understand about life through our experiences. The unfamiliar paralyzes us. So, we sit with a spirit instead of calling out to Jesus, who's resting in our boat. He's not the one who needs awakening. We are.

Mama, it takes courage to move forward in life after a loss as large as ours. I hear a lot of women say they won't ever move on from their child's death. It saddens my heart to know how broken they feel and to see that lack of hope in them that I felt throughout the final quarter of 2021 as the anniversary of Caleb's death approached. Rather than waking Jesus up, we sit in the storm with that spirit of grief. Instead of mustering up the name of Jesus in our hearts, we remain silent in our sadness.

It is time to move forward.

Survival Tip:

Mama, moving forward in life doesn't mean we leave our child behind. If we truly believe in Jesus as our Lord and Savior—and our child did—he or she is in our future, not our past. We must shift our focus from their death to their eternal life.

- **Acknowledge that it's good to move forward.**
  There is still an amazing amount of abundant life to live. God has you here for a purpose. He has plans for you that surpass your role as your child's mother. He is calling you to further His kingdom on earth until

He calls you Home too. It's time to shift your focus to walking out your faith and finishing your race.

- **Recognize that your child's race is run.** He or she is now in eternity and will not be returning to Earth. And that's okay. Consider the legacy your child left in the hearts of those who loved him or her. What aspect of their character do you cherish? How can you honor that in walking in obedience to Christ? In walking out God's plan for your remaining life?
- **Allow God to work His healing in your heart.** You will carry your child with you for the rest of your life. You don't have to carry the pain of grief with you. Give it to God. Ask Him to heal the hurt. Ask Him to mend the broken pieces and turn them into something that will glorify Him.

Mama, it's time to say goodbye to that spirit of grief and welcome joy back into your life.

A Verse to Focus On:

Why are you cast down, O my soul?
And why are you disquieted within me?
Hope in God, for I shall yet praise Him
For the help of His countenance.
Psalm 42:5

Reflection:

Somewhere deep inside of you, you know there are things God has called you to do. What are they?

surviving moving forward

CHAPTER 48

Trusting god with what remains

On New Year's Eve, Gideon was invited to hang out with some of his friends. This is a safe group of responsible young adults who have been spending time together since their junior year of high school (longer, probably—that's just when Gideon showed up on the scene). Under normal circumstances, I wouldn't hesitate to give him permission. But this year, it took everything within me to say yes.

As the first anniversary of Caleb's accident rolled up on us, I found myself facing all the what ifs.

...What if I had told him to drive carefully that day?

...What if we'd been home when he'd arrived that morning? Would I have had more time with him? Would he have been in a more joyful mood?

...What if he was still here? What would his life look like today?

...What really happened that night?

The fear of losing another child on a night infamous for drunk drivers had me talking to God for an hour before I could let my youngest son walk out the front door with his friends. I didn't want to let Gideon go.

But I also don't want to live in fear. Nor do I want to keep my kids from enjoying life because of my what ifs. As I prayed, God reminded me of the time He promised me He has them in the palm of His hand and will keep them close to Him. Ezra, Caleb, and Hannah were kneecap kids. Gideon was either a baby or in my womb at that time.

Because Vic and I had watched Caleb transform into a new being in his relationship with the Lord just prior to his passing, I knew I could continue to trust the Lord with all of my children. That He would keep His promise to draw them close to Him.

I cried a few tears as I hugged Gideon tight and told him to have a great time with his friends that New Year's Eve. He came home the next evening.

Mama, I know it's hard to let your kids go and trust God to take care of them. Especially if you've had to bury more than one child. We all wish we had control and could protect them from life and death. But the only one with that power is God. And it's something we have to come to terms with if we're going to take our foot off the brake and nudge the gas pedal. The light is green, and it isn't fair to hold back those who are following us because we're afraid of the next potential accident on this road of life.

Survival Tip:

Psalm 127 has brought me comfort over many years as my children grew. They were toddlers when God brought that chapter to life for me. This tip has more to do with our anxious hearts that worry about our children than something practical for us to do.

Psalm 127 begins with the truth regarding who is in control of life. *Unless the LORD guards the city, the watchman stays awake in vain.* It is clear that without God, everything we do is vanity. It's vanity to build our homes (i.e. serve our husbands, raise our kids, tend our households) and to stay awake, keeping watch until that teenager returns from his or her night out with their friends. Unless the Lord builds it first and guards our families.

It is also vain for us, in our grief, to rise up early, sit up late, and eat the bread of sorrows (instead of partaking of the Bread of Life). How many restless nights have you faced since your child passed, Mama? I can't count them on two hands, myself. This verse reminds us that God gives His beloved (that's you) sleep. So, if you're tossing and turning or feel you need to pace the floor when you should be sleeping, here are a few things you can do:

- **Post verses about God's plan for rest and sleep.** You can put them on the headboard of your bed or the nightstand next to it or the ceiling above it, where you can read them when you're unable to sleep.
- **Put on worship music.** Sometimes having something familiar to focus on helps me fall asleep faster, because it stills my thoughts.
- **Put on the Word.** YouVersion is a Bible app that has audible versions of the Bible. When choosing a version to listen to, look for the versions with the speaker icon next to them. Those are the ones with audio versions available.
- **Pray.** Pray God's blessings over your children. Peace over your household, your mind and heart.

The rest of the passage from Psalms goes on to remind us that our children are a heritage from the Lord. They are a reward.

I cannot—we cannot—worry about the children God has given us to train up in His ways. We cannot allow the enemy to rob us of precious sleep for fear of what may happen, despite what we've experienced thus far. Mama, we must trust God, the Creator of our children, the Father of our children, the One who loves our children on a level far greater than you and I can begin to comprehend. He has them in the palm of His hand, hidden under the shadow of His mighty wing. Who are we to worry?

A Verse to Focus On:

Unless the LORD builds the house,
They labor in vain who build it;
Unless the LORD guards the city,
The watchman stays awake in vain.
It is vain for you to rise up early,
To sit up late,
To eat the bread of sorrows;
For so He gives His beloved sleep.
Psalm 127:1-2

Reflection:

How has God shown you that you can trust Him? What's one memory you have where He protected or blessed you in a situation or circumstance that could have a far worse outcome?

CHAPTER 49

prioritizing and downsizing

One of the biggest regrets I have of parenting my kids is how much money I spent buying them toys, both during shopping sprees and for birthdays and Christmases. If I could go back and do it all over again, I would put that money into a college fund or save it for a rainy day or family adventure. They talk more about the camping trips we took than any object we ever bought them.

As I sorted through the few belongings Caleb had, I started to think of all the stuff in my house. How much of it was truly necessary? Did it really make me happy to own it? Or was it now a burden waiting for me to put it away or to move it so I could once again clean under and around it?

My priorities shifted as I figured out what to do with all of my son's things. I was acutely aware that our stuff doesn't go with us when we die. Instead, it remains for others to manage.

Relationships are what we take to heaven with us. We aren't going to be applauded by God for buying thoughtful Christmas presents. We're going to answer for every word and every deed we've done and how they affected others. How well we loved. The thoughtfulness and care we took to pick out that gift may matter, but the item will not.

Survival Tip:

Maybe you're feeling overwhelmed by all the things, Mama. Do you sort through your child's belongings now? Do you wait? Are you having trouble even entering his or her bedroom or home?

Maybe it's not even your child's things that have you overwhelmed. Maybe it's the stuff you've collected over the years that is making you want to crawl into bed and avoid the mental, emotional, and physical effort of cleaning out.

Here's what to do, whether you're cleaning out your house or your child's room:

1. **Buy four large bins.**
2. **Label each bin one of the following: trash, donate, gift, keep.**
3. **Take it one room at a time, giving yourself a week or two to go through each one.**
4. **Throw away all obvious trash first.** Then, as you go through the rest, be consistent with throwing away the things that you no longer want and are in poor shape or too personal to donate.
5. **Things that are in good shape can be donated.** You can take them to your local thrift store or do some research and find women's shelters, children's homes, and other charities to give them to.
6. **There may be some things you have that your children will want.** When I went through Caleb's items, I knew his siblings and friends would want his Lego sets that he'd built. His father and grandfather wanted his belt buckles. And there were a handful of items I wasn't willing to part with because they were a large part of who he was and what he enjoyed in life. Set these things aside until you can give them to the recipient, or invite your people to choose a set

number of items you're willing to part with. If anything remains, add it to the donation bin.

7. **Here are a few things to consider when deciding whether to add something to your keep bin:**

- Does this item bring me joy? If not, you probably don't need it.
- Does this item serve a particular purpose, and have I used it for that purpose in the past three years? If not, you don't need it.
- Have I worn that article of clothing in the past year? No? It's time to let it go.
- Can I scan that document, photo, or certificate and save it electronically in order to downsize my paper files?

You should be able to clean out your entire home within six months if you work at it consistently. If you still find yourself overwhelmed by it all, consider asking a trusted family member or friend to assist you. You don't have to do it alone.

Remember, you're making more space for relationships in your life when you declutter the stuff that keeps you too occupied cleaning up after it to spend time with those you love.

A Verse to Focus On:

"Do not lay up for yourselves treasures on earth, where moth and rust destroy and where thieves break in and steal; but lay up for yourselves treasures in heaven, where neither moth nor rust destroys and where thieves do not break in and steal."
Matthew 6:19-20

Reflection:

What "stuff" is taking up too much space in your life? In what ways did your priorities shift when your child passed?

CHAPTER 50

intertwined

One spring morning in 2021, Vic, Hannah, Gideon, and I drove around on a hunt for new living room furniture. The sun shone brightly in the sky after several rainy weeks, and I found myself joyful at the sight of it. Between stops at stores, we listened to some of our favorite—and Caleb's favorite—songs. We sang along as we always do, and I found myself sobbing deep sobs. Healthy sobs. Vic gripped my arm and gave it a squeeze because he knows, and he comforts.

Hours later, after finding a living room suite we could live with, we sat in a steakhouse, waiting for our food to arrive at the table. Out of nowhere, grief grabbed my heart and squeezed until tears streamed down my face again.

What was I thinking right then? How much joy it would bring me to see Caleb's headstone the next time I visited the cemetery, because after months of waiting, it had finally arrived. I'd been anxious to have the marker that tells strangers a little bit about my son and locates where he's buried. One second I smiled about it, the next I sobbed. Because I missed him so, so much in that moment.

Mama, some days, you'll be doing life, and grief will well up from within you like a geyser about to erupt. You may know what triggered it; you may wonder where it came from. It will steal your attention for ten minutes, thirty, a couple of hours. And then, as if someone turned off the water spigot, it fades back into the well of life. Your day will go on, and you'll survive.

Other mornings, you'll awaken with joy reverberating throughout the depths of your being as you anticipate what God is doing, filled with excitement over a new development in your life, or reveling in a relationship. On these days, you may find your memories are full of joy, not grief. Dare I say ... if you even consider your child on that day. I've had a day pass where my thoughts haven't drifted to Caleb. A few of them (though, not in a row), actually. Mama, this doesn't mean you've forgotten your child or don't love him or her anymore. It means you've come to a place of healing, and you don't have to wallow in your grief every day. Instead, you can access joy and delight in life again.

But more often than not, you won't experience one or the other in your days. Instead, *grief and joy mingle*, intertwined in the fabric of your life. Which seems odd but natural. Like wanting to laugh and cry at the same time. Like a bubble within that bursts, and you're not sure if you'll be soaked by its liquid or saturated in its wonder. The glory in this is that joy relieves grief's sorrow like honey on a bee sting.

Survival Tip:

Mama, here are a few ways to allow grief and joy to mingle in life after child loss:

- **Take note of what you're feeling.** Is it grief? Joy? Neutral?
- **Admit that it's okay to feel joy.** Doing so doesn't make you a horrible person, nor does it need to leave you feeling guilty.
- **When you notice that grief and joy are mingling, make note of it.** Write in your journal that despite

feeling your loss, you've also enjoyed this moment in your day.

A Verse to Focus On:

"O Death, where is your sting?
O Hades, where is your victory?"
1 Corinthians 15:55

Reflection:

What's one instance where you have noticed grief and joy mingling?

carry your cross

Mama, I'm writing this chapter three and a half years on the other side of my son's sudden death. I know it doesn't feel like it right now, but suffering is a gift. Without suffering, we wouldn't know healing. Without suffering, we wouldn't know comfort. Without suffering, we wouldn't know overcoming. Without Jesus' suffering and His death on the cross, we wouldn't know salvation and eternal life with our Father.

The Lord didn't promise us we wouldn't experience difficult things in this life. Instead, He told us to take up our cross daily and follow Him (Luke 9:23). Doing so means submitting our lives to God to the extent that we die to ourselves and our agendas, knowing that our relationship with God is the primary focus of life. That relationship comes before all else.

In Mark 10, Jesus tells the rich young ruler, who has obeyed God's commandments from birth, that he lacks one thing. He must sell all his possessions, take up his cross, and follow Jesus. The young lad's response? He went away sorrowful, because he had great possessions. What do you have that you feel you need to hold onto in the place of Jesus and your cross? Is it your grief? Your child? Something in your home?

Jesus tells His followers in Luke 14 that anyone who wants to be His disciple must hate their family members and even their own lives in order to do so. Does that mean we should leave our husband and abandon our children? Of course not. It means we make Jesus the priority in our home and our relationships. And if we suffer the loss of one of these, we don't allow our grief to overrule God's grace. In other words, we must be willing to lay down our life, pick up our cross, and follow Jesus. We must be willing to forsake all for Him.

Jesus also told us in Matthew 11:28-30 that He gives the laborers who are heavy with burden rest in Him. That His yoke is easy and His burden is light. I don't know about you, but some days, managing the grief of my children—or even my own—has me so weary I cannot focus on what God is calling me to do. Some days, the burdens of the heart stifle my ability to take up my cross and follow Him. *But Jesus.* There is so much we have to learn from Him.

Survival Tip:

So, what does carrying our cross look like when moving on in our grief journey?

Look for the lessons in the hardship. God didn't take your child Home to teach you a lesson. That's not what I'm saying. But in every hardship we experience, God can bring us into a new level of maturity in our relationship with Him if we allow His grace to show us His way through our grief.

I have discovered many new things about myself and my relationship with God throughout this journey. He has revealed deep-seated issues I've needed to work through that have kept me from deeper intimacy with Him for several years. I have also grown to know the width, length, depth, and height of God's love for me (Ephesians 8:13). Mama, there is so much to learn from this experience if you will open your heart to God. Grief doesn't have to rule your heart or your life. God's love for you will overrule grief if you allow it.

A Verse to Focus On:

But may the God of all grace, who called us to His eternal glory by Christ Jesus, after you have suffered a while, perfect, establish, strengthen, and settle you.
1 Peter 5:10

Reflection:

What's the hardest thing for you to admit to yourself and to God in this season of grief? What does God's Word say about that?

live to leave a legacy

If you were to look up the definition of legacy, you'd find it means a gift you leave someone by will, typically in the form of money or personal property. But when discussing leaving a legacy, we tend to consider what personal value we've left behind. How we've impacted others' lives. Not in a sense of accomplishment so much as in a sense of meaningfulness in relationships.

Caleb had an adventurous spirit. He faced life without fear. As a child, he could be found up a tree, herding crabs on the beach, or exploring off the beaten path while hiking. As a teen, he loved driving his car down back roads, eating grasshoppers and crickets, or camping out in the woods across the street from our house. He tried things he wanted to try without worrying what may happen. He went hard after life.

Caleb also loved others well. He cared deeply about his friends and family, and we knew it. Caleb gave the best hugs, which he called "squishies" when he was a toddler. Caleb's squishies were bony and sometimes hurt, he squeezed so tightly. But I knew he would never let go of me in his heart. Hannah remembers being on the way to a football game with him, and he'd stopped to buy her a blanket when she realized she'd dressed too lightly for the evening chill. His friends tell stories of how well Caleb listened and shared advice. They knew he loved them big.

If you knew Caleb, you knew he would talk nonstop if he got your ear. Mom and Dad took him for a day trip when he was little. He started talking the moment they got into the car to drive from Mobile, AL to Pensacola, FL to take him to the Air and Space Museum.

While at the museum, he acted as their tour guide, explaining all the planes to them, as he was also a lifelong learner, ever curious. His friends joke that he could tell you the history of a straight line. Seriously. Everything he said was intelligent, informative, and worth listening to.

Caleb's ambition was admirable. He'd received his student flight card in the mail just before his death. Didn't even get to open it. He was going to learn to fly. He'd also recently received the CDL manual from his boss. He was going to learn to drive the big equipment and trucks for the landscaping company. He had goals and dreams. Big ones. As you've read, he always went after them, never hesitating to accomplish the next thing.

While Vic and I miss our son every day, we've decided we'll seize every moment to love deeply and hold each other close in heart. Caleb would want us to live life to the fullest. To pursue our dreams, fulfill God's call, and finish this race well. We don't know how long we have left to multiply the talents God gave us and to glorify His name on earth, but we do know it's time to move forward and discover what adventures He has in store along the way.

Survival Tip:

Mama, I'd like you to do an activity for this final survival tip. One that I hope will help you step out of your loss and back into life.

I'd like you to write a legacy letter. Put on some music and light a candle, if it helps. Pour yourself a cup of your favorite beverage. Grab a few pieces of paper and something to write with, whether pencil, pen, or markers. It's important to write this in your handwriting rather than typing it on a computer. Your family will treasure the personal touch, I promise.

Follow the steps below to write your letter:

- **Start with your salutation.** (i.e. Dear, To my ..., Greetings loved ones)
- **In your first paragraph, write an explanation as to why you're leaving this legacy letter for your family and/or friends.**
- **Next, tell your story.** Avoid sharing all of your accomplishments. Instead, focus on who and what has impacted your life. What lessons have you learned from them? How did they help in the development of your character?
- **Share your values.**
- **Express gratitude for the people and events in your life.**
- **Share some of your regrets.** What would you choose to do differently?
- **Offer your readers blessings and guidance, but don't point fingers.** This is about you encouraging and inspiring them, not correcting them.
- **Sign your legacy letter.**

Now that you've created a handwritten copy, scan it into your computer and create a digital version for safe keeping. Add a copy of your handwritten version to your important documents. Finally, decide if you want to share it at the end of your life or after your death.

A Verse to Focus On:

The LORD will perfect that which concerns me;
Your mercy, O LORD, endures forever;
Do not forsake the works of Your hands.
Psalm 138:8

Reflection:

What do you want to be remembered for when God chooses to take you Home?

acknowledgments

Because I will always seek You first in all I do, Lord Jesus, I first thank You for Your love, comfort, and grace. This life and this book would be impossible without You.

Victor, I am grateful that when God created a man for me, it was you. Your encouragement to get this book out of me and into the world has been a blessing. I'm grateful for your never-ending support, love, and faithfulness to me and our children.

Zachary, Ezra, Victoria, Hannah, and Gideon, I'm grateful that God has blessed me with each of you. Thank you for making my life worthwhile. I cherish every one of you.

Mom, thank you for being my biggest cheerleader. I wrote a book! Dad, thank you for your continual belief in me. Love you both!

Frieda and Lief ... as you wish ...

Shawnna and Beth, thank you for holding space with me. I love you both more than I could ever put into words.

Lynette, DiAnn, Edie, Ramona, and C.J., thank you for your abundance of insight and encouragement as I wrote and wrote and rewrote. Y'all are the best!

Blythe, thank you for your recommendations and your steadfast support of my efforts. I appreciate you!

To all the mamas who've provided feedback along the way, I cherish you. I pray God blesses you with comfort, peace, and joy as you get one day closer with every sunrise and sunset. Thank you for blessing me with your kind words, keen eyes, and assistance in making this book something beautiful.

To my Advance Team, thank you. Thank you. Thank you. I could not have gotten this into the hands of these precious mamas without you! Y'all rock!

And to all my friends and family who have encouraged me and asked about how the book is coming and told me you couldn't wait to read it or gift it to another mama, I am forever grateful God blessed me with you in my life. His love shines through you all every day.

To Vincent B. Davis II and Heather Kreke for all the self-publishing advice and answering my myriad of questions.

And last but not least, thank you to those who made this book beautiful:

To Hannah Linder of Hannah Linder Designs for the gorgeous cover. To Courtney Hopkins of Tiny Pine Art for bringing the seasonal tree I had in my head to life. To Mom for suggesting the addition of Caleb's wind chimes to the tree. And to C.J. for the idea of the tree when I was struggling to come up with a cover concept that would set this book apart from others on the shelf. To Lisa DeLelys, sister-in-law and graphic artist extraordinaire for the A Word In Season Publishing Company logo design, as well as help with one of the photos I included in "Caleb in a Cloud."

notes

Chapter 7

1. Sarah Haufrect, "The Mental Health Benefits of Strength Training," *Psychology Today*, July 25, 2018, https://www.psychologytoday.com/us/blog/the-bonds-we-make/201807/the-mental-health-benefits-strength-training

Chapter 12

1. "Kintsugi," Wikimedia Foundation, Last Modified July 3, 2024, 12:54, https://en.wikipedia.org/wiki/Kintsugi

2. Tiffany Ayuda, "How the Japanese Art of Kintsugi Can Help You Deal with Stressful Situations," BETTER by TODAY, Updated April 28, 2018, 08:59AM, https://www.nbcnews.com/better/health/how-japanese-art-technique-kintsugi-can-help-you-be-more-ncna866471

Chapter 18

1. Alexandra Benisek, medically reviewed by Melinda Ratini, DO, "Why We Cry: The Truth About Tearing Up," WebMD, July 7, 2022, https://www.webmd.com/balance/features/is-crying-good-for-you

Chapter 19

1. Sanjana Gupta, medically reviewed by Sabrina Romanoff, PsyD, "What to Know about the Denial Stage of Grief," verywellmind, Updated November 22, 2023, https://www.verywellmind.com/the-denial-stage-of-grief-characteristics-and-coping-5272456

Chapter 20

1. Lisa M. Shulman, MD, FAAN, "Healing Your Brain After Loss: How Grief Rewires the Brain," American Brain Foundation, September 29, 2021, https://www.americanbrainfoundation.org/how-tragedy-affects-the-brain/

Chapter 23

1. Alikay Wood, "What Does It Mean to Dream about a Deceased Loved One?" *Guideposts*, https://guideposts.org/angels-and-miracles/miracles/gods-grace/what-does-it-mean-to-dream-about-a-deceased-loved-one/

Chapter 31

1. T. Stewart, *Overview of motor vehicle traffic crashes in 2021* (Report No. DOT HS 813 435), National Highway Traffic Safety Administration, April 2023, https://crashstats.nhtsa.dot.gov/Api/Public/ViewPublication/813435

2. South Carolina Department of Public Safety. (2021). South Carolina Traffic Collision Fact Book. https://scdps.sc.gov/sites/scdps/files/Documents/ohsjp/fact%20book/2021%20Fact%20Book%20Final.pdf

Chapter 32

1. Grace H. Christ, D.S.W., George Bonanno, Ph.D., Ruth Malkinson, Ph.D.,

Simon Rubin, Ph.D., Institute of Medicine (US) Committee on Palliative and End-of-Life Care for Children and Their Families; Field MJ, Behrman RE, editors, *When Children Die: Improving Palliative and End-of-Life Care for Children and Their Families*, "Appendix E: Bereavement Experiences after the Death of a Child," National Academies Press, 2003, https://www.ncbi.nlm.nih.gov/books/NBK220798/

about the author

Alycia Morales has been writing for over a decade and has been published in multiple compilations, devotionals, and various online and print publications. Her mad editing skills have helped hundreds of clients win various awards. In her role as book coach, she loves helping authors improve their writing craft and polish their manuscripts for publication. She also teaches at writers conferences across the United States.

Alycia is an ordained minister through Faith Connect, under Apostle Robert Engelhardt. She loves leading small groups and speaking on marriage, parenting, and encouraging women of faith to live abundant, joy-filled lives in Christ.

She lives in South Carolina with her husband and is adjusting to an almost empty nest. When she makes the time to do so, she enjoys hiking, taking scenic rides (with camera in hand), painting, reading, and binge-watching favorite shows. Although she loves sweet tea and sugary coffee drinks, she's given up sugar and switched to unsweet tea and black coffee. The brain fog is lifting...

For more valuable content from Alycia, please visit her website at www.alyciawmorales.com.

facebook.com/AlyciaWMorales

x.com/AlyciaMorales

instagram.com/alywmorales

Made in the USA
Columbia, SC
17 September 2024

42460338R00122